Houseplants

Which Plant to Choose According to Lifestyle

(Unlock the Secrets to Bringing Nature Indoors and Transforming Your Living Space)

Jeremy Adams

Published By **Phil Dawson**

Jeremy Adams

All Rights Reserved

Houseplants: Which Plant to Choose According to Lifestyle (Unlock the Secrets to Bringing Nature Indoors and Transforming Your Living Space)

ISBN 978-0-9947564-6-6

No part of this guidebook shall be reproduced in any form without permission in writing from the publisher except in the case of brief quotations embodied in critical articles or reviews.

Legal & Disclaimer

The information contained in this book is not designed to replace or take the place of any form of medicine or professional medical advice. The information in this book has been provided for educational & entertainment purposes only.

The information contained in this book has been compiled from sources deemed reliable, and it is accurate to the best of the Author's knowledge; however, the Author cannot guarantee its accuracy and validity and cannot be held liable for any errors or omissions. Changes are periodically made to this book. You must consult your doctor or get professional medical advice before using any of the suggested remedies, techniques, or information in this book.

Upon using the information contained in this book, you agree to hold harmless the Author from and against any damages, costs, and expenses, including any legal fees potentially resulting from the application of any of the information provided by this guide. This disclaimer applies to any damages or injury caused by the use and application, whether directly or indirectly, of any advice or information presented, whether for breach of contract, tort, negligence, personal injury, criminal intent, or under any other cause of action.

You agree to accept all risks of using the information presented inside this book. You need to consult a professional medical practitioner in order to ensure you are both able and healthy enough to participate in this program.

Table Of Contents

Chapter 1: Benefits Of Indoor Gardening . 1

Chapter 2: Low-Moderate Houseplants . 17

Chapter 3: Tropical Plants 30

Chapter 4: The Micronutrients Of Fertilizers 43

Chapter 5: Winter Fifty Seven 57

Chapter 6: Common Troubles And Troubleshooting 67

Chapter 7: Popular Houseplant Varieties 81

Chapter 8: Planting And Potting 95

Chapter 9: Maintaining Healthy Houseplants 109

Chapter 10: Indoor Plant Decor And Display 124

Chapter 11: Advanced Houseplant Care 138

Chapter 12: Nurturing Your Green Thumb 145

Chapter 13: Even Rescue Your Houseplants 159

Chapter 14: Basic Care For Any Houseplant 162

Chapter 15: The Wonderful World Of Propagation 182

Chapter 1: Benefits Of Indoor Gardening

Having an indoor garden can carry some of benefits for each you and your private home. Not best will it help make your living region look extra lovable, but it also brings many different incredible results.

Gardening indoors is peaceful and calming, just the smash from each day lifestyles that you need! It may additionally even decorate your intellectual and bodily health in some tremendous strategies. So in case you've been trying to pursue greater interests, why not get some flowers and strive out indoor gardening? Here are some reasons why having an indoor garden is a wonderful concept!

Improved air splendid

Do you comprehend the strategies plants assist us? Plants act as natural air purifiers. They absorb carbon dioxide and supply us smooth air to respire through freeing oxygen. And a few plants may even easy out risky pollutants from normal gadgets like carpets and furniture. This permits you breathe much less complex in your living areas.

Increased humidity

By releasing moisture into the air, flowers may be very beneficial in dry climates or any form of indoor vicinity that will be predisposed to warmness up speedy. Having plants in your home or elsewhere gives you an exceptional benefit of having easy, herbal humidified air all round for you and your own family to get snug and comfortable in. Being able to take a deep breath with the proper humidity in the surroundings is a brilliant-of-existence improvement you didn't comprehend you desired!

Mental nicely-being

If you're seeking to beautify your temper, lessen strain and growth productivity, you can want to don't forget getting yourself some plants! Gardening promotes neuroendocrine and affective recovery from stress (Van Den

Berg, Custers, 2011) shows that interacting with flora ought to make a large distinction.

Not handiest that, having plants in your property is the ideal way to hold a chunk of nature indoors, which can be extraordinary for those individuals who don't have the luxurious of having our outdoor garden or outside. Furthermore, it's an easy and a laugh hobby that calls for minimal attempt and maximum satisfaction!

Increased humidity 9

Learning revel in

Gardening is a superb manner to discover new matters, even from your private home! By looking after vegetation, you may discover more approximately the kinds of plants that exist, how specific species want particular care, and the first rate conduct of diverse plants.

This statistics can be exciting and it feels wonderful when your plants are wholesome and thriving!

There's not anything quite much like the pleasure of correctly developing your own leafy flora or plant life.

Best of all, it's not a interest you want to do on my own if you don't need to. You can percentage vegetation together with your pals and family, cope with vegetation at the side of your kids, or maybe brighten a person's day, if not week, with colorful houseplants.

Psychological benefits of indoor gardening

Are you organized to study the entire first rate intellectual advantages of indoor gardening? Beyond absolutely being pretty to have a test, houseplants may have a large excessive great effect to your intellectual nicely-being! Studies have located that gardening can assist raise our moods and decrease stress degrees. According to The affect of vegetation on productivity: A crucial evaluation of studies findings and test strategies (Bakker & van der Voordt, 2010), popular plant care also can enhance interest and productivity too! With this in mind, permit's take a higher have a look at every of these high-quality benefits in extra element.

Stress bargain

Interacting with plants may be calming and can even assist lessen pressure! Taking care of your flora may be a pleasant little spoil from the anxiety of era. That damage is right for us in greater methods than one, like supporting lower our cortisol tiers, that is our "stress hormone". Caring for plant life has been connected to those exceptional consequences, so why not deliver it a attempt?

Improving mood

Taking time to take care of indoor vegetation may have superb benefits for your emotional properly-being! Not brilliant can the surroundings grow to be extra calming, however a blooming flower can also moreover even provide you with a revel in of accomplishment.

But that's no longer all: traumatic for a residing organism, which incorporates an indoor plant, has been known to generate feelings of empathy and positivity. Fresh flowers look stunning in any home and provide a extremely good way to keep your intellectual fitness in accurate form through using presenting an interest that rewards a while of rest.

So subsequent time wintry weather comes knocking, hit up your nearby nursery; except fireplace conversations or tv shows on name for, the present of nature can be clearly what you need!

Boosting awareness and memory

Studies have proven that having flowers in our surroundings can acquire this a good buy more than sincerely brighten up the region! They can decorate interest and reminiscence. Our reputation and productivity boom via up to 15 percentage if we hold foliage inner our location of view, be it our domestic or workspace. So why not beautify your place of work or look at location with some lush flora?

Encourages mindfulness

Taking up indoor gardening is an a laugh manner to workout mindfulness meditation. As you attend on your flowers' needs, like watering, pruning, and studying for pests, it lets in you to stay centered on the venture to hand, letting you (quick) forget about about any pressure you may probably have at that 2d.

By paying attention to the wishes of your plant life, you could find that this particular relationship benefits every of you in techniques you in no way predicted!

Boosting recognition and memory thirteen

Essential device and substances

No revel in essential! Indoor gardening is a fun and worthwhile hobby, and it doesn't must be complex. All you need are a few primary equipment and resources. Here are the necessities:

Pots and bins: A domestic on your plants. Make fine there are drainage holes to save you waterlogging.

Soil : Different flora have one-of-a-kind soil alternatives, however a contemporary indoor potting mix will paintings for maximum plant life. Watering Can: For watering your flora. Some encompass an extended spout for clean get admission to to the vegetation.

Pruning Shears: For trimming and keeping your flora.

Fertilizer: To provide your plant life with the essential vitamins.

Light Source: If you don't have enough natural light, you may use a increase light.

Ideal indoor environment

Creating an appropriate vicinity for an indoor plant is a whole lot much less complicated than you may assume. Keeping temperatures among sixteen-24°C (60-seventy five°F) and a humidity diploma of about 40-60% will positioned your flowers within the consolation area! Most homes are already within the proper temperature and humidity variety, so that you possibly gained't ought to trade a element.

If your home is a hint too dry, you can however keep your plants glad. Misting flora or the usage of a pebble tray is an easy way to maintain the humidity up. You could also use a humidifier, it definitely is remarkable for offering more moisture even as wished.

Good air move lets in too. However, avoid placing your flowers in warm or bloodless drafts, like near air con devices and home domestic home windows. Most flora don't do properly in drafts, so a place with a steady temperature and humidity is incredible.

And that's all there can be to creating a wonderful indoor surroundings for max houseplants. Now permit's have a examine what you need to look for with regards to daylight hours.

sixteen Ideal indoor surroundings

Light necessities for houseplants

Light is important for any plant's increase and survival. Your vegetation photosynthesize after they get sunlight, which lets in to feed them. This technique identifying clearly ho

w an entire lot sunlight hours your indoor plants need is essential to retaining them healthful and pleased.

Knowing the brightness of the sunlight hours your plant likes and the manner prolonged they need to spend inside the sun offers you tremendous clues approximately finding the right location in your house for your plant. Do they choose spending time close to a window or do they prefer a darker nook of the room? This is important statistics to preserve your vegetation glad.

Let's have a look at the wonderful types of sunlight hours and notice which varieties of plants do terrific in which sort of daytime.

Direct daytime

Direct daytime is the pleasant for masses varieties of plants, like succulents and cacti. It's after they get to take in all of the sunlight hours without some thing blockading the sun's rays. But you mustn't overdo it!

Not all plants love the solar. Most houseplants choose staying out of direct mild due to the fact an excessive amount of have to burn their leaves and be bad to them. Most houseplants are tropical plant life that broaden beneath tall wood in the jungle. This is in which they get hundreds of daylight hours, however it's usually filtered via the wood above.

If you're going to place your houseplant in some direct daylight, make certain you hold a watch fixed on how it does, so you can address it and ensure that it flourishes!

Indirect moderate

Indirect mild, moreover called "filtered" moderate, approach that the sunlight hours is not proper away hitting your plant. Most houseplants, along facet Pothos or Monsteras, in fact pick this type of lighting!

You can get oblique moderate interior through placing a thin curtain a few of the window and your plant or simply putting your plant in regions in which sunlight hours by no means reaches your plant at once.

So is direct daylight hours continually bad for these types of plant life? No! If you've were given a great spot near a window wherein your plant doesn't get any direct sunlight hours for the duration of the most up to date a part of the day, you could use that spot for a plant that prefers indirect sunlight hours.

Most vegetation will do simply terrific in the occasion that they get a few direct daylight within the early morning and past due afternoon or early night. This sunlight is often now not strong sufficient to motive any harm in your plant. Make great to test your plant often even though and flow it if it's despite the fact that getting burn marks.

Low moderate

No sunlight, No problem! Low-slight vegetation can despite the fact that thrive in areas which have minimum sunlight hours. Are you thinking which flora to pick for those darker spots? Well, no want to worry because of the reality Snake Plants and ZZ Plants are every splendid

Low slight 19

low-mild plant picks. These, and other, forms of plants can live on in locations without too much harsh mild from domestic windows or lamps. So why now not supply your updated dim and relaxed areas a colorful contact with some low-slight houseplants?

These low-slight flora frequently expand very slowly and is probably pretty low protection. The darkish corners of your private home don't need to be stupid.

Choosing the right houseplants

Finding the right houseplant to name your own may be just like finding a latest pal! Each plant has a wonderful individual and picks, just like we do. Doing a few research and locating the only that fits your own home and way of existence should make all of the difference, every as regards to looking after the plant and its health!

Whether you could promise loads of sun and area or simplest a small corner within the residence, there's a plant on hand that feels without a doubt proper for you. Let's discover how you can pick out the right houseplants in your indoor garden.

Understanding the sunlight hours in your house

Are you within the marketplace for a trendy plant? If so, there's one essential detail to hold in mind: the lights situations in your own home. You need to get it in reality right, otherwise your plant might not be able to draw sufficient energy from the environment and received't be capable of attain its entire capability!

To make sure that your plant is flourishing, make the effort to assess how an entire lot slight the space has and research some plant life that would do properly in that place. After all, no quantity of care can repair wrong lighting situations.

Take some time to take a peek spherical your house at brilliant instances of the day! You'll have a take a look at plenty approximately in which the mild is coming from and really how superb it is.

South-going through home windows normally get the most spots of light, at the same time as north-managing domestic domestic windows have the least. If you get east and west home home windows in your own home then you definitely absolutely'll be in desirable fortune due to the truth they provide a first-rate balance!

Keep in thoughts that direct mild is immediately from the sun, with none filters, and can be too sturdy for masses indoor flora. While oblique moderate is superb as it's though super and tremendous with out being overwhelming or too excessive on your houseplants!

We've already looked at the styles of sunlight hours, so now I'd need to offer you a few plants that you can bear in mind for your dwelling areas for the one of a type types of mild. These flora are all newbie-top notch and could make your dwelling space even better.

Chapter 2: Low-Moderate Houseplants

If you've discovered that your dwelling area doesn't get an entire lot of natural mild, don't fear. Many flora thrive in low-slight situations. Here are a number of them, along facet pointers on a way to attend to them:

Low-mild houseplants 23

Snake Plant (Sansevieria)

Known for its tall, striped leaves, Snake Plants can continue to exist in low-light situations and don't need to be watered frequently.

ZZ Plant (Zamioculcas Zamiifolia)

ZZ Plants are hardy and may tolerate low moderate. They moreover prefer to be on the dry side, so be careful now not to overwater.

Peace Lily (Spathiphyllum)

The Peace Lily has appealing foliage and white flower spathes. It has prolonged, drooping leaves which might be oval and characteristic a dark inexperienced shade with white veins. It likes to be watered a piece more frequently and might make bigger cute flower-like white leaves.

When annoying for low-mild flowers, recall that "low moderate" does not advise "no mild." They though need a few slight to broaden, so location them in a niche that gets indirect mild. Also, because of the truth they expand more slowly, they don't need as plenty water or vitamins as plants that get more mild.

Bright, indirect sunlight houseplants

If you've discovered that your residing location receives a few direct sunlight hours inside the early morning or overdue afternoon and is within the (partial) shade during the hottest part of the day, you is probably seeking out a plant that likes indirect sunlight hours. Let's check a few novice-first-rate options.

Philodendron

With their coronary heart-formed leaves, Philodendrons do well in low to colorful, oblique moderate and like continuously wet soil.

Pothos (Epipremnum aureum)

Pothos are some of the hardiest houseplants and may thrive in

Bright, indirect daylight houseplants 25

low or vibrant, indirect light. They decide upon soil that stays lightly wet but no longer soggy.

Spider Plant (Chlorophytum comosum)

Spider plants have prolonged, grass-like leaves with white stripes and make a first-rate addition to any domestic. They need colourful, indirect moderate and calmly wet soil.

When it involves houseplants that like colourful, indirect slight, maintain in thoughts that they despite the fact that need quite a bit of mild, simply no direct daytime in the afternoon. Place your plant in a place that gets partial color for optimum of the day and placed it near a window so it could get sufficient mild to thrive.

Direct mild houseplants

If you've determined a gap that's within the full sun in the course of the afternoon, you'll want to search for vegetation that thrive in direct daylight hours. Let's check some amateur-best flora on the way to do properly in direct daylight hours.

Succulents

Succulents are to be had in lots of sizes and patterns, from small rosettes to massive timber. They need masses of direct sunlight hours and require well-draining soil that doesn't live too wet.

Cacti

Cacti are exceptional for folks who want flora that don't require a

Direct mild houseplants 27

lot of preservation. They want hundreds of direct moderate and prefer soil that drains fast.

Aloe Vera

Aloe Vera is a popular houseplant for its recuperation homes. It desires brilliant, direct slight and barely dry soil.

When seeking out flora that do properly in direct daylight, don't neglect about to offer them a while to regulate in advance than leaving them in direct sunlight hours. Start thru giving them some hours of morning sun and often increase the amount of time they spend in direct mild so that you can slowly adjust to their new home.

No rely what kind of lights you've got were given have been given in your own home, there are masses of flowers so that you can thrive. I desire the ones guidelines will give you some thoughts for regions that would be brilliant for those one-of-a-type kinds of plant life.

Factors to endure in thoughts while selecting flora

When selecting houseplants, there are elements extra than truely mild situations to don't forget! Perhaps you don't have masses of time to spend to your plant life, you continuously forget to water your flowers, or you have got have been given pets. Let's check a few sensible factors to study at the same time as getting a plant.

Maintenance

Some plant life require more care than others. If you're new to plant care or have a busy lifestyle, choose flora which may be smooth to take care of. If you'd like to take care of your plant a piece extra regularly, virtually to have a damage in the direction of the day, look for plant life that need to be watered a touch extra often.

Pet Safety

Some flowers may be toxic to pets. Always test if the plant is safe when you have furry friends at domestic. In the following section, we'll have a check some guidelines for flowers that are steady to have round pets and small youngsters.

Size

Before deciding on out a plant, examine the size of the gap you have. How a whole lot stretching room do you discovered flowers need? Believe it or no longer, some vegetation can grow to be massive! If you need to fill that vacant spot to your dwelling room, don't forget about about to recall how big your plants can boom earlier than you even pick them up!

Humidity

Some vegetation require greater precise care to thrive. Many tropical flora love a wet weather. Achieving this shape of environment

Factors to undergo in thoughts while selecting flora 29

interior can be complex at instances. So it's right to check whether or not or now not or no longer the plant may be a notable healthful for the space and in case you're inclined to move the greater mile to make the plant sense at home.

Matching the proper plant on your living area is already half of of of the artwork of supporting it thrive. If your plant feels at home, it'll be thousands much less complicated to attend to than at the same time as you need to take extra steps to enhance the growing environment.

Pet-secure and infant-stable vegetation

If you proportion your house with pets or younger youngsters, it's important to pick out flora which can be solid for them. Did you realize that pretty some well-known houseplants may be poisonous if ingested? Petals and leaves of those plant life have to cause symptoms beginning from infection to even extreme health problems.

The proper records is, you don't ought to fear approximately this problem in case you do your studies and get a few non-toxic houseplants. Let's have a look at a few accurate options.

Spider Plant (Chlorophytum comosum)

The spider plant is a notable desire for individuals who need to start with houseplants however are worried approximately toxicity. It is one of the few vegetation which may be honestly secure for pets and small kids.

Areca Palm (Dypsis lutescens)

Areca Palm is the proper plant for pet proprietors and people with children! Its leafy fronds twist into lovely, cascading arcs making any place sense like a tropical paradise.

Boston Fern (Nephrolepis exaltata)

Ferns are non-poisonous to pets and people. They opt for a fab environment with immoderate humidity, making them excellent for lavatories or kitchens.

Swedish Ivy (Plectranthus verticillatus)

This fast-developing plant is secure for pets and youngsters. Its

Pet-stable and toddler-secure vegetation 31

cascading vines make it perfect for placing baskets.

Baby Tears (Soleirolia soleirolii)

With its touchy, cascading leaves, Baby Tears is safe for pets and children. It prefers a wet environment and can be used in terrariums.

These flowers are in reality harmless in case your pets or kids through chance devour them and they're also pretty clean to take care of. However, it's normally an tremendous concept to educate younger kids to address plants cautiously and make certain your pets don't devour your plants. This will educate them to stay far from plants that might be toxic inside the future.

Watering your flowers

Watering is one of the most crucial elements of plant care, however it's additionally one of the trickiest. Give too little water and your plant could likely wilt; provide too much and it would rot.

The same goes for the soil - it's no longer pretty a good deal providing an area for the roots, however additionally about giving your flora vital nutrients and drainage.

Let's dive into knowledge the watering goals, choosing the right soil, and gaining knowledge of the superb watering techniques in your indoor plant life.

Watering desires for incredible plant types

Plants may appear all of the same, but it's pretty extraordinary how unique they will be! Every kind of plant has its non-public watering desires, based absolutely totally on every its herbal habitat and how the plant grows. So to make sure your flora have become just enough water, right here are a few beneficial popular recommendations you can comply with for maximum sorts!

Succulents and cacti

These drought-loving flowers need far an awful lot much less water than other vegetation. Make sure to attend till the soil has dried out surely before watering them. How lengthy it takes in advance than the soil has certainly dried out relies upon on some matters, but on common this ought to be once every 14 days in the summer season and as quickly as each 21-30 days within the wintry weather.

You can test if the soil is completely dry thru choosing up the pot and feeling its weight. This takes a hint little little bit of exercising, but you come to be pretty exquisite at this after some tries. You can work out through feeling the load right when you've watered your plant and comparing that to the burden after 14 days.

Chapter 3: Tropical Plants

Tropical flowers, which incorporate ferns and orchids, normally will be predisposed to opt for immoderate humidity levels. Watering more frequently will help maintain the soil moist but now not soaked. It's time to water the ones kinds of flora whilst the pinnacle 1-2 inches of the soil has dried out.

You can take a look at whether or no longer the pinnacle of the soil is dry via sticking your finger inside the soil and seeing if the little debris keep on together with your finger or resultseasily fall off. If they fall off without issues, the soil is dry and you're organized to water your plant.

On common, you need to water these plants as quickly as in line with week within the summer season and as soon as each 10-14 days within the iciness. Always take a look at if the top of the soil is dry earlier than watering your plant

Watering dreams for one-of-a-type plant sorts 35 even though.

Watering your plant life inside the fall and winter

It's additionally essential to word that some vegetation might in all likelihood want more or lots much less water relying on the season. For example, in some unspecified time in the future of the wintry weather months, most vegetation will want much less water than throughout the summer season.

Tips for correct watering strategies

Now which you recognise at the same time as to water your flora, it's time to discover the excellent manner to obtain this! Let's appearance and be conscious how we are able to supply them the hydration they need.

Water thoroughly

When it's time to water, make certain you water the soil till water starts offevolved offevolved to escape out of the drainage holes at the lowest of the pot. Don't fear in case you water it too much, that's what the drainage hole is for.

When the water starts offevolved offevolved to drip from the lowest of the pot, it manner that the moisture has reached the roots of your plant life. When the water begins offevolved to drip from the bottom of the pot, you may permit the greater moisture from the pot for 5-10 minutes. You can do this in a sink to avoid creating a massive quantity in your private home.

After 10 mins, the soil has tired any extra moisture and you've flawlessly watered your plant.

Avoid moist leaves

When watering your plant, try to avoid getting water on the leaves and recognition on watering the soil as a substitute. This can forestall the formation of fungal illnesses that frequently spread with wet leaves. If you do display as much as get some drops of water on the leaves, definitely wipe them off with a mild fabric.

Temperature topics

When watering your plant life, it's crucial to apply roomtemperature water! To check the temperature, you could refill

Tips for proper watering strategies 37

the watering can earlier in order that the water can sit down for a few hours. That way, at the same time as it's time to offer them a drink, it'll be honestly right!

You need to use room-temperature water to save you beautiful the plant's roots. Water that's too warm or too bloodless can damage the roots and result in root rot.

Watering frequency

Different flora have distinct water necessities, however a substantial rule of thumb is to water them each 7-10 days inside the summer season and as soon as each 14-21 days in the wintry climate.

Checking the soil earlier than watering your plant is the fine way to find out if the plant wishes water or if it's however doing exceptional and goals a few extra days.

Overwatering vs. Underwatering

One of the maximum commonplace problems that indoor gardeners face is overwatering. You'll apprehend if this has happened if the leaves have become yellow or are wilting. Overwatering your vegetation can cause root rot, that might kill your plant.

This is why I usually suggest checking whether or now not or not the pinnacle of the soil is dry earlier than you water your plant. This clean step earlier than giving your plant a fantastic soak will prevent your plant from getting too much moisture.

On the opportunity hand, every so often you neglect approximately about to water your plant for some time. It can appear to definitely everyone, but it's a good buy a exquisite deal much less in all likelihood than overwatering your plant. If you be conscious brown, crispy leaves and a unhappy-looking plant, you may want to water your

Overwatering vs. Underwatering 39

plant a piece extra frequently. Most plants will bypass right all over again to their colourful self once you've watered them.

Choosing the right potting blend for indoor flora

Plants want the proper form of soil to help them boom robust and wholesome. And fortunate for us, there are masses of types of soil to pick out out from! Are you looking to repot your plant on every occasion speedy? Here are some options you can wanna don't forget.

General indoor potting blend

This type of soil is appropriate for optimum indoor vegetation. It's designed

General indoor potting combo forty one

to preserve sufficient water for the plant while though draining properly. It additionally has the right quantity of nutrients to help your flowers thrive. It generally consists of great materials to help maintain the soil mild and fluffy. This form of soil is meant for vegetation that need to dry out in amongst waterings.

Cactus and succulent soil blend

Cacti and succulents require what's called a "rapid-draining" blend due to the fact they select drier situations than different houseplants. This form of soil won't keep an excessive amount of moisture for too prolonged, giving your succulents and cacti the quality environment to thrive.

Tropical soil mix

A tropical soil mixture is a mixture of a preferred soil aggregate with peat moss, and sand or perlite. This shape of mixture is designed to hold pretty a chunk of moisture for some days, drain more moisture rapid, provide your flowers with masses of nutrients, and live moderate and ethereal. This can be very essential for those flora that favor to amplify in soil that's wet most of the time, because the moisture tends to compact the soil over time.

forty Choosing the proper potting mix for indoor plant life

Flower mixture

If you're seeking out soil that'll deliver your flowers the greater some detail they want, then this is it. The flower combo is enriched with nutrients to help boom blooming and flowering in positive kinds of houseplants. This soil isn't suitable for lots different flowers as its very whole of nutrients and holds masses of moisture.

Orchid mix

While orchids are technically plants, they've very unique soil requirements. These varieties of flowers don't truly expand in the soil however on the bark of trees. This is why you gained't find (masses of) soil in an orchid combo. The orchid blend usually includes woodchips, as that is closest to how the ones plants may additionally develop in their herbal habitat.

When choosing a potting mixture, make sure it's appropriate for the plant you're potting. The shape of soil has a big impact on the plant's nicely-being. For instance, growing succulents in soil that's supposed for flowers will overwater the plant right away. The succulent goals very dry soil.

If you're unsure of which soil must be used with which plant, you can normally ask professionals at your close by garden shop or look up the awesome kind of soil inside the plant care publications on

 plantcareforbeginners.Com.

Flower combination 43

Nutrients and Fertilizers

Nutrients are an crucial a part of lifestyles for each plants and humans. Just like we depend on a balanced eating regimen for our health, increase, and power, vegetation want vitamins to live strong and thrive too!

Sure, plants have to make their food the usage of photosynthesis, however that doesn't suggest they don't despite the fact that require all the vitamins that may be discovered in soil. Without treasured nutrients from the earth, plant life may also need to struggle to live on.

Unlike plants grown in the wild which have plenty of soil to take in nutrients, houseplants fine get their vitamins from a restricted amount of soil in their pot. Without those important vitamins, your plants received't be developing as wholesome as they have to! But don't worry, fertilizers are right right right here to assist.

Let's examine more about plant nutrients, fertilizers, and a manner to apply them efficiently.

Understanding plant vitamins

When it involves growing big and sturdy, plants want severa exceptional vitamins. These vitamins are divided into two groups: macronutrients and micronutrients.

This subsequent section may sound complicated, but happily the fertilizer producers have achieved most of the difficult artwork for us and made particular mixes. If you're now not interested in the technical explanation of fertilizer, you could skip to the following segment about the only of a kind kinds of fertilizer.

The macronutrients of fertilizers

Macronutrients are essential for keeping plants healthy, and there are three fundamental ones. Nitrogen (N), Phosphorus (P), and Potassium (K) are the trio of macronutrients that art work collectively to provide the electricity your plant life want to thrive. When you're searching out recommendation on fertilizer, you will probable pay attention or examine approximately their acronyms referred to as NPK. When it comes time to buy fertilizer, keep an eye constant out for the NPK code, it looks as if a fragment together with 10-10-10 or 2-three-four.

This NPK code method the proportions of those macronutrients inside the fertilizer product. So what do those proportions endorse precisely? Let's have a examine what every of these macronutrients brings to the desk and feature a look at it to a meal:

Nitrogen (N) is just like the plant's predominant route - it permits the plant expand loads of inexperienced leaves. So, when you have a leafy plant or if you want your plant to develop large and taller, you'd want a fertilizer with a higher first variety.

Phosphorus (P) is similar to the dessert - it allows with flowering and fruiting. If you're developing vegetation which you need to bloom masses of plant life or fruit, a better center amount will be better.

Potassium (K) is like a drink - it enables the plant stay healthful trendy, helping it fight off ailments, tolerate the cold or drought, and distinctive critical functions. If you want a plant to be really sturdy and wholesome, you'd search for a better very last variety.

If you're stressed, no problems, fertilizer producers have done their manner and make unique mixes which may be very easy to apprehend by the use of the label, like "Cacti fertilizer", "Orchid fertilizer", "Green leaf fertilizer", and "Tropical plant fertilizer". This makes it plenty a lot much less hard to get the proper fertilizer.

Chapter 4: The Micronutrients Of Fertilizers

Micronutrients or trace elements are small however important on your plant's fitness. That's why they need to have just the proper quantities of elements together with iron, manganese, and zinc.

Did you understand that if your vegetation don't get enough of these vitamins, they assist you to understand? A loss of nitrogen can purpose yellowed leaves at the same time as not having sufficient phosphorus must result in sluggish boom and undeveloped flowers and fruit.

It's an extraordinary idea to keep a watch in your plant life so that you can spot any troubles like nutrient deficiencies early. The faster you come across a deficiency and cope with it with the right

micronutrients, the better off your flowers may be!

Let's provide an reason behind the micronutrients within the equal manner we did the macronutrients:

Iron (Fe) is like Vitamin C for plant life. Just like how Vitamin C facilitates our our our bodies stay wholesome and heal faster, Iron helps vegetation create chlorophyll, which they want to make their meals.

Manganese (Mn), Zinc (Zn), and Copper (Cu) are like Vitamin D, E, and K. They every play a function in outstanding additives of the plant's growth, like assisting it use exceptional nutrients extra correctly or helping it produce seeds.

Molybdenum (Mo) and Boron (B) might be the least recognized, however they're nevertheless very vital. They assist vegetation use Nitrogen and also help with flower and seed production.

Again, in case you're uncertain what to do with this statistics, the fertilizer manufacturers have had been given your once more. They add the ones micronutrients to the fertilizer and have finished all the tough work for you.

Different styles of fertilizers

Fertilizers can are available in all patterns and sizes! Knowing a chunk greater about the professionals and cons can help you in jogging out which type might be better applicable on your state of affairs. Let's check a few precise varieties of fertilizer.

Granular fertilizers

These gradual-release fertilizers are a terrific way to make sure your plants get all the nutrients they need through the years! Just add them to the soil even as you repot your plant and they'll deliver the wished nutrients for severa months. During this time, you acquired't have to consider fertilizing your flora anymore.

Most of these sluggish-launch fertilizers will feed your plant for a hundred days. So you may workout them while you repot your plant inside the early spring and you gained't ought to fertilize your plant again till the summer time.

Liquid fertilizers

Adding fertilizer to the water at the same time as you're giving your flora a drink is a first rate way to provide them the more vitamins they want! Just blend the fertilizers into the water and it right onto your plant's soil. Your plant life will take in the vitamins brief, so that you'll need to try this more regularly: as quickly as every 2 to 4 weeks is proper. That way, your flora will live nourished and happy!

Different kinds of fertilizers 40 nine

Spikes or tabs

Fertilizer tabs and spikes are a amazing way to make sure your plant gets all of the nutrients it desires for healthy increase! All you need to do is push the spikes or tabs into the soil and, over time, they'll dissolve and launch those critical nutrients and minerals.

After you've added the ones spikes or tabs to the soil, make certain to water your plant to assist spread the vitamins during the pot.

These spikes or tabs will, just like the granular fertilizers, last round 100 days. So if you've repotted your plant within the early spring and added the fertilizer to the soil, you may stick 1 or 2 of those within the soil at the start of the summer time and you've fertilized your plant for the entire 12 months.

When you follow fertilizer on your houseplants, normally use houseplant fertilizer for indoor plants, as those are in particular made for flowers that develop interior.

They offer your plant with more nutrients that out of doors flowers mechanically get from rain or dust particles in the wind.

Outdoor fertilizer is usually a bargain greater focused as nicely and not appropriate for houseplants. By the usage of outdoor fertilizer, you could overfertilize your plant and harm its roots.

Fertilizing schedules

So how regularly do you need to fertilize your flora? Well, that is predicated upon on 2 subjects: your plant and the fertilizer you've gotten. Most flowers want to be fertilized every 2-four weeks, but some want a chunk extra or much less fertilizer than others. If you're unsure, test the label in your fertilizer for instructions: it'll permit you to realize at the same time as and what form of to use.

Growing season

Spring and summer time are the most important times for plant life! During the developing season, they want masses of nutrients, so make sure to fertilize frequently. You'll discover specific instructions on each fertilizer package deal, so sincerely have a have a look at via the ones and also you're suitable to move! Giving your flora hundreds of electricity at some stage in this time will help them live wholesome and strong.

Dormant season

As the cooler months of fall and winter technique, severa your flowers may additionally have lots much less want for fertilizer and can even pass dormant. That's why it's vital to offer them simplest what they want.

Fertilizing schedules 51

If you're too generous at the aspect of your fertilizer sooner or later of dormancy, pretty a few salts inside the combination will stay within the back of within the soil. Over time, the ones salts can create an environment that's no longer healthful for flora. So don't overlook about to suppose twice at the same time as including fertilizer in autumn and winter, your vegetation will thanks for it!

Overfertilization or "root burn"

Fertilizers are complete of vitamins that vegetation want and frequently come in the form of salts. When we offer a plant an excessive amount of fertilizer, it's like dumping some of salt onto the plant's roots.

The roots of your flowers soak up moisture within the pot very much like consuming water with a straw, so if there can be an excessive amount of salt within the soil it makes soaking up the water pretty tough.

All of those salts don't absolutely make it tough to absorb the water, but they're able to actually start to soak up moisture that's already within the roots. This reasons the roots to get "burned", what we commonly name "root burn".

So what are you able to do at the equal time as this takes place? You can flush the salts out of the pot with the useful resource of giving your plant a deep soak. You try this thru way of setting the pot with drainage holes inside the sink and watering your plant with a watering can.

This is high-quality even as watering your plant typically. When you water your plant normally, you forestall watering it at the same time as extra moisture starts offevolved to drip out of the drainage hole. When you flush the salts out, you acquired't prevent even as it starts offevolved to drip from the drainage hollow, instead, hold going till the watering can is empty. The salts need to be flushed from the pot for your plant on the way to heal.

Overfertilization or "root burn" fifty three

Seasonal contend with indoor flowers

As the seasons alternate, so does the surroundings of indoor flora. Even even though inner vegetation are included from masses of outside climate, they notwithstanding the truth that revel in modifications. These modifications can affect how they enlarge and stay healthy.

To assist our plant life stay the healthiest, we want to be aware of such things as mild, temperature, and humidity tiers in our houses. Let's test what looking after our vegetation looks as if at some point of the seasons of the three hundred and sixty five days.

Spring

Is it getting a piece hotter? That can best endorse one issue: your vegetation are waking up from their wintry weather shut eye! In the spring, your flowers emerge as alive. They begin to grow and bloom, the whole house will come alive.

To help your vegetation stay healthful in the route of this season, begin thru manner of along side a few extra water to the soil and start to fertilize your vegetation again.

The spring is one of the remarkable instances to repot your plant life because of the truth they'll heal and get higher fast. Be top notch to offer your flora a pot that's slightly large and upload clean, nutrient-wealthy soil to get your plants organized for explosive growth within the spring.

Summer

During the maximum updated season of the yr, many plant life apprehend extra humidity to get them through the day! You can attempt grouping exceptional types of plant life in a unmarried area or placed your flora on top of a tray entire of pebbles and water. Misting your flowers is likewise a exceptional way to raise the humidity spherical your plants.

During this warmness season, ensure to move a number of your flora some distance from the home windows. The harsh and heat sunlight will cause

Spring fifty 5

sunburns on those plants that don't like direct daytime.

You can understand a sunburn through searching out the ones signs:

1. Leaf scorch: The leaves might in all likelihood begin to look bleached, diminished, or whitish in the middle. Or they will flip yellow or brown, in particular spherical the edges or in between the veins of the leaves.

2. Brown or Black Spots: These seem like small, crispy brown or black spots on the leaves, however they will expand if you don't seize them in time.

3. Wilting or Drooping: Even even though it looks like the plant is getting masses of daylight hours and water, a sunburned plant may probably appearance wilted or droopy. This occurs because of the fact the extra sunlight can harm the plant's functionality to absorb and use water well.

4. Drying or Crisping: If the sunburn is excessive, the leaves should likely come to be very dry, crispy, or perhaps start to crumble even as you touch them.

Autumn

As the times get shorter, you can word your indoor flowers start to gradual down. That's okay! There are techniques to assist them flourish as the season modifications. One manner is reducing their water consumption and prevent fertilizing your plant.

You may additionally need to transport some of your indirect moderate flora toward the window. It's darker outside, so what end up their first-class spot in the summer season is now a spot that appears more like a low-moderate spot.

Winter

Lots of flowers generally take a destroy in a few unspecified time within the future of the bloodless wintry climate season. That way indoor flora particularly would probable want an entire lot lots much less water than ordinary and no fertilizing the least bit while they're in this dormancy period.

If there isn't an awful lot light round your house, try giving them a few greater doses of light or artificial moderate! Just be cautious not to location them too close to cold domestic home windows that would reason them to too bloodless.

During the winter you're probably also turning at the vital heating another time, so the air inner of your own home becomes very dry. It's nicely to take measures to boom the humidity round your flowers within the period in-between.

Chapter 5: Winter Fifty Seven

Common houseplant pests

Looking after indoor flora is a laugh – but every now and then, even with your quality care, you could face a few problems. What form of troubles? Well, most often pests, diseases, or environmental stressors are in price.

Let's check some of the most commonplace pests and the way we are capable of address them to help keep our indoor lawn wholesome and happy for a long time.

Spider mites

Spider mites are tiny, 8-legged bugs which is probably very hard to grow to be aware about with the naked eye. One of the correct strategies to identify spider mites to your flowers is if you begin to see what seems like cobwebs. Spider mites are tiny insects, but their webs are pretty clean to become aware of. They will start to appear on the stems on leaves of your plant.

The spider mites themselves can despite the fact that be observed for your plant despite the fact that. They'll look like tiny dots that may be yellow or brown. They commonly want to cowl on the bottom of leaves and motive damage thru poking tiny holes in flowers' leaves to suck out the sap. One of the number one signs of spider mites is the appearance of tiny, mild-coloured spots on leaves.

Spider mites 59

You can manage and eliminate spider mites in numerous one in every of a type techniques. Your first option is to apply a regular circulation of water to flush them off the plant. You can also use insecticidal cleaning soap or neem oil to suffocate them. It's vital to spray the plant over and over to make sure you get all of the mites and their eggs.

Mealybugs

Mealybugs are tiny, white, cotton-like bugs that attach themselves to the stems and leaves of your houseplants. They feed on plant sap, that might cause stunted increase and harm to the leaves.

You can commonly discover those insects in businesses around the stem, leaves, or in the difficult-to-attain areas of plants. They produce a white, waxy substance that makes them appear to be small cotton balls and makes them smooth to end up aware about.

Mealybugs thrive in heat and humid environments, which is probably the proper growing conditions for quite some tropical plant life interior as nicely. Mealybugs can unfold effects from plant to plant, so it's important to seize them early and take action to govern their populations before they get out of hand.

To control mealybugs, use a cotton swab dipped in rubbing alcohol at the insects to suffocate them. Alternatively, a few people use horticultural oils like neem or vegetable oil, which smother the bugs. Make effective to copy this way every few days until the infestation has died.

Mealybugs 61

Scale

Scale insects may be difficult to recognize due to the fact they appear on leaves and stems as small, flat bumps. They can decide your houseplant because of severa motives like overfertilization, lack of daylight, overwatering, and excessive humidity. These hard-to-spot pests are interested by prone and compelled flora, and they feed at the sap, inflicting harm and weakening the plant in addition.

To add to their inconveniences, these pests moreover produce a sticky substance referred to as honeydew that draws ants into your garden!

To put off them, it's critical to prune and get rid of the affected additives of the plant proper away. You can use insecticidal cleansing cleaning soap or neem oil to suffocate the dimensions insects as properly. If you're looking for a gentler approach, use a smooth-bristled brush or sponge to wash away at them.

It may additionally take multiple applications of this elimination technique over some days in advance than all of the scale bugs had been removed.

Fungus gnats

Fungus gnats are tiny, black, or dark gray flies that fly round your houseplants. They lay their eggs inside the soil. When the larvae hatch, they'll feed to your plant's roots and specific herbal material within the soil. These larvae weaken your plant via feeding on its roots, which makes it vulnerable to different pests.

Luckily, man or woman fungus gnats don't cause any damage to the plant

Fungus gnats sixty three

itself, but their presence can be disturbing. These adult gnats are interested in wet soil, so if you constantly overwater your plant, you can trap those gnats. A remarkable manner to save you that is through letting the soil dry out for a day earlier than watering your plant again.

If fungus gnats have already infested your plant, you may control the infestation by way of converting the pinnacle layer of soil with easy, dry soil. If the infestation is certainly too huge, you may additionally use chemical insecticide to kill the larvae in the soil.

A extra natural way to eliminate these larvae in the soil is to introduce little worms to your plant. These worms, additionally referred to as nematodes, will feed on the larvae and the eggs, so will indirectly do away with the gnats for you.

Aphids

Aphids are tiny bugs that suck the sap from houseplants, inflicting them to wither and die. They're effortlessly recognizable because of the fact they cluster collectively on the stem and undersides of leaves. They are to be had in excellent colors, like inexperienced, yellow, brown, pink, or black, but the maximum commonplace is green.

Like mealybugs, aphids thrive in warmness and humid

environments. You can regularly discover them in overcrowded and poorly ventilated areas, in addition to on vegetation which have been too moist for too prolonged.

Aphids can spread from plant to plant, specifically if the plant life are close to collectively. They can also be carried from one plant to every other thru bugs, people, or with the resource of moving inflamed soil or

Aphids sixty 5

plant cloth. This is why it's essential to regularly test to your plants and ensure you lure aphids early to prevent too much harm.

To manage aphids, you can use a consistent motion of water to flush them off your plant.

You also can use insecticidal soap or neem oil to suffocate them. If you're searching out an ecofriendly answer, you could get some ladybugs that will help you out. Ladybugs are herbal predators of the aphid, so introducing them into your plant can be an powerful way to manipulate the infestation.

Whiteflies

Whiteflies are tiny, white, moth-like insects that suck the sap from the leaves of houseplants. They're a very common pest in greenhouses, however also can start to assault your houseplants. Whiteflies, irrespective of the decision, moreover may be yellow, not definitely white. They could probably appear like moths but are greater related to aphids.

Whiteflies reason leaves to expose yellow and fall off. Whiteflies are tough to manipulate because of the fact they lay their eggs on the bottom of leaves and then fly off, making them difficult to intention.

To manipulate whiteflies, use a yellow sticky lure to capture the adults. You also can use insecticidal cleaning cleaning soap or neem oil to smother them. For extreme infestations, use a chemical insecticide that you combination with water and pour into the soil. Your plant will absorb this and kill the whiteflies when they feed on it on the plant's sap.

A outstanding manner to prevent whiteflies from choosing your plant is to maintain the leaves moist with the aid of often misting them. Whiteflies sixty seven

Thrips

Thrips are tiny, slim bugs that feed at the sap of houseplant leaves and plant life. They're difficult to perceive for your plant life because they're most effective 1-2 millimeters lengthy. Thrips are available special colorings, along with black, brown, and yellow. They seem like spider mites, but won't depart any of the cobwebs within the decrease returned of.

Thrips purpose harm via manner of scratching the leaf floor and sucking the sap out of the plant. When thrips feed on your plant's sap, it may sluggish the plant's growth and turn the affected leaves yellow and brown.

Thrips are evidence towards maximum types of chemical insecticides, which makes them tough pests to get rid of. However, there are numerous tactics to govern the infestation. You can use insecticidal cleansing soap or neem oil to suffocate them, however you may moreover introduce predatory mites, like Amblyseius Cucumeris and Amblyseius swirskii, to control the population.

A brilliant way to prevent and manage the infestation is through often wiping your plant's leaves and stems. This keeps the plant freed from dust and receives rid of any bugs which can be currently at the plant. Make positive to prune any useless or loss of life leaves, because of the reality thrips are inquisitive about them.

Chapter 6: Common Troubles And Troubleshooting

Now that we've looked at common pests, allow's have a study exceptional common problems that you may probably notice for your vegetation.

Root rot

When it consists of ailments, overwatering can bring about some frightening and uncomfortable fungi like root rot. If you begin to see a few element off collectively together with your flowers, you can have overwatered them.

Symptoms of an overwatered pot may additionally encompass yellow or brown leaves or perhaps comfortable spongy ones. You can with out issue prevent overwatering your plant with the useful resource of way of double-checking the moisture in the soil in advance than watering your plant.

Temperature and humidity

Indoor vegetation often battle with dry air, in particular sooner or later of wintry climate even as the warm temperature is on. To boom humidity, you could location a tray of water near your flowers, mist them frequently, or use a humidifier. Also, keep away from placing flora near radiators or air con vents, as these can create dry conditions and unexpected temperature fluctuations.

unexpected temperature fluctuations.

seventy five°F). Sudden adjustments can motive stress, so try to maintain the temperature regular.

Be particularly careful while putting vegetation close to home windows, as glass can increase the warm temperature in summer season and allow in bloodless drafts in wintry weather.

Recognizing signs and symptoms and symptoms of pressure

Plants can show you when they're sad, but you could need to exercise a touch to understand the symptoms. Keep an eye fixed constant out because a healthy plant will show minor signs and symptoms of misery that might not be without troubles seen. Here are some commonplace signs:

Yellow leaves

Seeing yellow leaves can be a hint alarming, but don't fear! That doesn't suggest a few components drastic has took place. It may want to simply endorse that your plant has been overwatered, or perhaps it's getting too much solar. It's moreover possible that your plant isn't getting sufficient of positive nutrients.

Brown, crispy leaves

Are your plant's leaves looking a chunk brown and crispy? This might be the cease cease end result of underwatering or a reasonably low humidity diploma. Be fantastic to check the soil and water your plant if wanted. You can trim the brown, crispy leaves.

Wilting

Have you determined your flora wilting? There are commonly viable motives for this: overwatering or underwatering. The clue to locating out which one it's far may be determined in the soil. If the soil is dry, your plant dreams greater water. If the soil is wet or moist, you have to drain the extra moisture and permit the soil dry out.

Slow growth or small leaves

Are your plant's leaves a chunk small, or is it growing slowly? It might be time to offer your plant some extra hobby. Maybe it needs more slight or the right form of vitamins.

Propagation strategies for indoor vegetation

Are you prepared to take your indoor gardening adventure to a latest level? Propagation, the gadget of growing new plants from seeds, cuttings, or other plant factors, is a notable way to find out how plenty you've already discovered out approximately searching after plants! You received't absolutely be nurturing present plant life but growing cutting-edge ones too.

Propagation through cuttings

Did you know that most of the plant life you want, like pothos and philodendrons, may be cloned through taking small cuttings? You can amplify an entirely new plant from handiest a small piece of the triumphing plant.

Before you get commenced out, pick a more potent, greater healthful stem and ensure there are numerous leaves on it. That's important due to the fact they'll distribute power to the decreasing even as it's developing roots. Snip off your piece of the 'determine' plant cautiously.

After you take your cuttings, you get a "toddler" plant! The very subsequent component to do is to vicinity your plant into a box of water until it grows roots. During this era, it's critical to be affected individual and offer the little one plant with the proper situations for root improvement. A warm spot with oblique slight is usually excellent. Be nice to exchange the water frequently to preserve it clean and keep a watch out for roots.

Once roots have grown, you could float your decreasing to a small pot with soil. Once you've planted the lowering in soil, you've began growing an entire new plant and also you've efficiently propagated your plant.

Propagation through cuttings seventy five

Propagation with the resource of branch

Some flora, like snake plants and peace lilies, grow in clusters that may be divided into severa person plants. You can separate the ones plants from every one in all a kind by means of the use of taking the entire plant out of the pot and the use of a easy, sharp knife to reduce the flowers off every other.

After you've separated a cluster into severa person flora, you could placed every in their pot and also you've efficiently propagated your plant thru department.

Propagation through leaf cuttings

Did you apprehend that some plant life, like succulents, have an brilliant capacity to grow an entire new plant from just one leaf? This fantastic machine is referred to as propagation via leaf cuttings.

Here's the manner it really works: you cautiously do away with a leaf out of your plant, letting it dry and heal for a few days. This drying way is essential, because it prevents capability damage whilst the leaf starts offevolved its rooting system.

Once dried, you genuinely lay the leaf on pinnacle of the soil. Be affected character, as that is wherein nature plays its miracle! In due time, the leaf will sprout roots or maybe a tiny new plant. This is probably the suitable manner to propagate a plant.

Propagation via leaf cuttings 77

Repotting and Transplanting

Just like us, flowers may additionally furthermore outgrow their houses every every now and then and need a bit greater location to extend. Or, every now and then they sincerely deplete all the nutrient strengths from their soil.

That's why plant life want room to maintain developing their roots. Repotting is the method of giving your plant a fresh begin in a modern-day, roomier home, with a glowing deliver of nutrient-rich soil. But how can we do that?

Here are a few steps to examine on the same time as repotting your vegetation: 1. Choosing the proper pot: When your plant is ready for a ultra-modern domestic, ensure to pick out out a brand new pot that's in reality one or sizes huge than the present day-day one. Going too big can result in overwatering issues, which could harm your plant. You need to offer your plant a bit extra room, however no longer loads that it gets out of location!

2. Picking the proper soil: Every plant has its alternatives in phrases of soil. Use a clean potting blend appropriate in your precise plant kind. This will supply your plant all of the nutrients it desires to thrive in its new home.

3. The shifting technique: Gently do away with the plant from its antique pot, taking top notch care now not to damage its roots. It may be a bit of a wonder for a plant to transport residence, so the gentler you may be, the higher.

four. Settling proper into a modern day home: Now, vicinity your plant in its new pot. Fill the distance throughout the roots with your preferred potting mixture, ensuring to move away a bit bit of area on the top for watering.

5. The first watering: Just like you will probably water the lawn after laying down new grass seed, it's essential to water your plant very well after repotting. This enables the plant settle in and moreover makes certain the modern soil is frivolously wet.

Remember, repotting is a piece like moving house on your plant. It can be annoying, but it's also an exciting opportunity in your plant to hold growing and thriving. With these tips in hand, you'll be well-organized to assist your plant life thru the shifting procedure.

Plant grooming and preservation

Taking care of your flora with normal grooming and maintenance is truly as essential as searching after your pets! This kind of steady attempt can maintain your flowers searching super, but it additionally permits guard them in opposition to illness and encourages strong growth. Plus, there are lots of a laugh belongings you get to do while demanding to your vegetation! Let's dive into unique steps for retaining your plants happy and wholesome.

Dusting

Dusting 81

Keeping your indoor flora clean can play a crucial function in their fitness. Dust accumulates on leaves through the years, clogging their pores and impeding photosynthesis, so preserving the ones strength plant life satisfied begins offevolved with periodic dusting!

For huge leaves, attempt wiping them down with a tender damp fabric. For plant proprietors with plant life that have smaller leaves, obtain for a clean brush or a twig bottle to make the leaves dirt free.

Pruning

Taking care of your plant with pruning is essential to maintain it looking healthy and beautiful! Pruning lets in preserve the shape, encourages bushier growth, and receives rid of useless stems and leaves.

When you're equipped, capture multiple sharp scissors or pruning shears. Where need to you chop? Look for a leaf node, the area in which the leaf connects to the stem. That's your best access! Prune just above it for the brilliant effects.

Deadheading

It's clean to assist your flowering houseplants! Deadheading is a smooth gardening method in order to have them looking lovely in no time. All you want to do is pinch or reduce off the blooms when they've dwindled away. Just ensure to be cautious no longer to damage each different factors of the plant on the identical time as you figure. This will help enhance new blooming, so that you can enjoy your colorful houseplants all all once more!

Rotating

Plants generally generally tend to glaringly grow in the direction of the slight, that would reason them to emerge as lopsided through the years. There is a manner to cope with this: frequently rotate them so their boom remains symmetrical. Moving your plant round will make sure that every factor gets same sun publicity and facilitates inspire "even" increase.

Inspecting for pests

Deadheading eighty three

You want to regularly check your flowers for signs of pests. Have a have a look at the underside of their leaves and take a peek alongside the stems. Take be privy to any damage or pests you spot.

Being capable of entice any pest infestations as early as possible can prevent a whole lot of trouble down the street. Preventing an infestation is the right manner to assist your plant stay wholesome.

Taking care of your indoor flowers can be an fun interest and a super opportunity! Grooming and upkeep are vital for retaining your plant life wholesome. Doing plant care is not simplest useful but calming too! Each time you do it, it could experience like a amusing mini-second of connection with nature. Don't forget about to revel in the process; there's nothing better than seeing your plant life thankfully thrive because of your love for taking care of all of it.

Chapter 7: Popular Houseplant Varieties

three.1 Succulents and Cacti

Due to their amazing and alluring appearance and relatively minimal upkeep needs, succulents and cacti are popular alternatives for houseplants. These plants are ideal for indoor developing because of the reality they've got advanced to flourish in arid conditions.

Succulents:

Plants called succulents may additionally additionally withstand dry environments via storing water in their leaves, stems, or roots. They are a fave among plant aficionados because of their outstanding form of shapes, sizes, and sun sunglasses. Succulents are to be had in loads of famous types, which incorporates Echeveria, Aloe, Haworthia, and Sedum.

Caring for Succulents:

Light: The majority of succulents choose direct, sturdy light. It is great to region them near a window that allows filtered mild. However, extended exposure to sturdy, direct sunshine can scorch their leaves.

Soil: To stop root rot, it's far essential to have nicely-draining soil. Use a shop-bought succulent blend or make your personal with the aid of which include perlite or sand to standard potting soil to sell drainage.

Watering: Succulents do not want to be watered often. Between waterings, allow the soil certainly dry out, after which water deeply, ensuring the more water drains away. Underwater is typically most useful to overwater.

Temperature: The majority of succulents flourish in temperatures among 60 and 75 °F (15 to 24 °C). Although they have to be included from frost, they might bear slightly decrease weather.

Cacti:

A subset of succulents called cacti is splendid via its function appearance, which includes spines and a specific boom shape. Native to the Americas, they may range in length and shape from tiny spherical kinds to tall columnar ones like the well-known Saguaro cactus.

Caring for Cacti:

Light: Cacti want robust mild, similar to succulents. In contemporary, they thrive in direct sunlight hours. If you're growing them indoors, offer them as a good deal daylight as you could by manner of placing them via a south-dealing with window, for instance.

Soil: Cacti opt for a soil combination that drains properly. There are business cactus mixes available, or you could beautify drainage with the aid of which includes sand or perlite to traditional potting soil.

Watering: Despite having a completely unique water garage tool, cacti do not require a bargain irrigation. Before watering, permit the soil absolutely dry out. Water extra often sooner or later of the developing season (spring and summer season), however less often at a few stage in the dormant season (autumn and wintry climate).

Temperature: Warm temperatures are usually favorable for cacti. They can tolerate more temperatures during the day but choose cooler temperatures at night time time, that is just like their real barren vicinity domestic.

Succulents and cacti are each low-protection plant life, making them fantastic options for novice gardeners and time-pressed people. It's vital to hold in mind that distinctive species also can have one-of-a-type care wishes, so it's miles a superb concept to investigate the excellent necessities of the succulents and cacti you've got were given for your collection. These thrilling plants can carry a chunk of the barren area into your own home and deliver you years of a laugh with the right upkeep.

three.2 Leafy Greens: Ferns and Foliage Plants

A massive fashion of non-flowering flora, which includes ferns and foliage flora, are essential for giving each indoor and outdoor settings splendor, texture, and depth. These flora are nicely-preferred selections for gardens, landscapes, and interior ornament because of their lush, inexperienced leaves. Let's discover some vital fern and foliage plant dispositions:

Variety and Types:

There is a large form of sizes, shapes, and textures to be had for ferns and foliage flowers. One of the oldest plant households, ferns are distinguished by manner of their sensitive and feathery fronds. They can also stay to inform the tale in a number of settings, from dry rock gardens to humid, sheltered woodlands. Boston, Maidenhair, and Bird's Nest ferns are a few common sorts of ferns.

On the possibility facet, foliage vegetation encompass a massive form of non-flowering plant life renowned for their appealing leaves.

Snake Plant, Pothos, Calathea, and Dracaena are different famous foliage flowers. These plant life are extensively sought-after for ornamental functions because of the fact they often display complicated patterns, variegated leaves, and numerous shades.

Caring for Ferns and Foliage Plants:

The health and energy of ferns and foliage flowers depend upon proper care. Here are some fashionable protection recommendation:

Light: Indirect or filtered mild is desired with the useful useful resource of maximum ferns because of the fact direct daylight can harm their fragile leaves. Different foliage flora require high-quality amounts of moderate; some can tolerate low moderate ranges even as others choose out direct, extreme moderate.

Watering: In brand new, ferns determine upon soil this is often damp but not soggy. Water necessities for foliage plants range;

some need soil this is continuously moist at the same time as others select to dry out amongst waterings. Striking a balance is critical if you want to save you root rot or dehydration.

Humidity: Higher humidity is beneficial for lots ferns and foliage plants, particularly the ones which can be local to tropical areas. Making the precise weather might be aided thru using misting or using a humidity tray.

Soil: Ferns and foliage vegetation both require properly-draining soil. To help generate the ideal soil conditions, mix potting soil, perlite, and peat moss together.

Fertilization: During the developing season, ordinary fertilization can inspire robust improvement. Use a fertilizer this is water-soluble, balanced, and designed for houseplants.

Benefits:

Beyond their seen appeal, ferns and foliage flora have a number of benefits:

Air Purification: Numerous foliage flora paintings nicely as air purifiers, disposing of pollutants and enhancing indoor air incredible.

Stress Reduction: It has been installed that the presence of greenery lowers pressure and could boom emotions of well-being.

Interior Décor: Foliage plants may be imaginatively covered into indoors format to enhance it through way of giving rooms more texture, colour, and brightness.

Biodiversity: Ferns and extraordinary foliage vegetation can offer safe haven and food to lots of insects and unique tiny animals in outdoor gardening.

Landscaping and Design:

Ferns offer an airy and peaceful factor to gardens that are shaded or in wooded region settings. They may be used on the aspect of other plants that thrive in shadow to make lush, layered landscapes. Due to their numerous appearances, foliage plant life are adaptable in terms of layout. They may be included into combined plantings, used as solitary focal regions, or perhaps used as indoor centerpieces.

In conclusion, because of their one-of-a-kind splendor and beneficial functions, ferns and foliage vegetation are important to horticulture, landscaping, and interior format. They are viable alternatives for each pro gardeners and novices wishing to infuse their environment with herbal splendor due to their capacity to flourish in numerous environments.

three.3 Blooming Beauties: Flowering Houseplants

Any indoor environment might advantage from having flowering houseplants for the purpose that they supply colour, heady scent, and vibrancy. These vegetation add to the cultured appeal of your private home at the identical time as also bringing a enjoy of calmness and nature within. A thorough list of indoor flowering vegetation is furnished beneath:

Types of Flowering Houseplants:

Orchids: Orchids are valued for his or her delicate beauty and supply prolonged-lasting blooms in severa sizes, shapes, and hues.

African Violets: These small, furry vegetation have sensitive, vibrant plants and require little renovation.

Peace Lilies: Peace lilies thrive in low mild conditions and additionally serve to clear out the air manner to their attractive white blooms.

Begonias: Begonias are available in a substantial range of kinds and include colorful leaves and extraordinary flora.

Geraniums: These conventional flowering flora, which frequently seem in outside gardens as nicely, have clusters of colorful blossoms.

Jasmine: Jasmine plants produce tiny white blossoms and are well-known for his or her lovable perfume. People experience their olfactory appeal.

Care Tips:

Light: The quantity of slight that flowering flowers need varies. Others fare well in low-moderate settings, while some thrive in direct, remarkable light.

Watering: Watering well is essential. Underwatering could make blossoms wilt, on the same time as overwatering would possibly bring about root rot. Recognize the specific necessities of your plant.

Humidity: Tropical and orchid flowering flora, specially, want higher humidity levels. Utilizing a humidity tray or misting can be useful.

Temperature: The majority of indoor flowering plants enjoy constant temperatures without massive swings.

Soil: For a plant to grow healthily, a potting combo that drains well and meets the dreams of the plant is important.

Fertilization: During the growing season, everyday feeding permits sell wholesome flowering. Pick a fertilizer that is balanced or one made for floral flowers.

Maintenance:

Pruning can promote extra plant life and hold a compact shape thru manner of having rid of wasted blossoms and lowering lanky increase.

Support: To hold their stems right away, some flowering plant life, like hibiscus, may additionally want stakes or other facilitates.

Repotting is occasionally vital as vegetation mature and outgrow their pots. When the plant's roots develop congested, repot it to provide it with new vitamins and room.

Keep a glance out for traditional pests like mealybugs and aphids. Check your plant life often, and if an infestation is positioned, take motion.

Challenges:

Flower Drop: When their habitat or care regiments change, a few flowering indoor plant life might also additionally moreover lose their buds or blooms.

Fungal ailments may be as a consequence of overwatering or insufficient air go with the waft. Address any sickness signs proper now.

Limited Bloom Time: The period of the flowering time may additionally vary counting on the species. But with time, with the right care, more vegetation also can seem.

Decorative Value:

Living rooms, bedrooms, workplaces, and kitchens all experience the natural splendor that flowering houseplants bring to numerous indoor areas. Their severa colorations and aromas add to the mood of an area, fostering a slight and aesthetically appealing environment.

Understanding their unique necessities and supplying the ideal care are crucial for incorporating flowering houseplants into your interior décor. With the proper care, those vegetation might also additionally offer months of adorable blossoms and a enjoy of nature's wonderment interior your own home.

Chapter 8: Planting And Potting

four.1 Transplanting and Repotting

Repotting and transplanting are vital techniques for maintaining the increase and health of indoor flowers. They encompass shifting a plant with sparkling soil from one discipline to any other, typically a bigger one. These strategies beautify nutrient absorption, provide the plant more room to increase, and prevent it from turning into root-certain.

Reasons for Transplanting and Repotting:

Root Boundness: A plant evaluations awful increase and nutrient absorption while the roots outgrow their cutting-edge vicinity and grow to be root-sure.

Compaction and nutrient depletion of the soil in a discipline can show up over the years, impeding the increase of the plant.

Improved Growth: The plant has more room to increase and spread its root system while transplanted into a bigger area with new soil, which results in thicker foliage and higher flowering.

Management of Disease and Pests: Repotting lets in you to examine the roots and do away with any infected or infested regions.

Larger pots can provide taller or top-heavy plant life extra balance and beautify the plant's popular aesthetic attraction.

Signs Your Plant Needs Repotting:

The plant's roots have encircled the pot's edges, causing it to grow to be root-sure.

Due to its excessive weight, the plant frequently topples over.

After watering, the soil right away dries out, indicating that it cannot maintain moisture.

The plant seems stunted and its increase has stalled.

The quantity and period of the leaves or plant life both quite decline.

The drainage pores at the bottom of the sphere are displaying symptoms of root growth.

Steps for Transplanting and Repotting:

The maximum fine time to transplant is commonly in the spring as it coincides with the developing season.

Choose a New Pot: Select a pot with a diameter that is 1-2 inches large than the satisfactory you have got were given already have been given. Make notable it has openings for drainage.

Get the plant prepared: Before transplanting, water the plant for an afternoon or two. As a stop result, the plant might not enjoy pressure and can be much less complicated to take out of the pot.

Turn the pot upside-down at the same time as laying your palm over the soil to gently take away the plant. To loose the plant and its root ball, tap the pot's base.

Examine the Roots: Gently untangle any looping or tangled roots, and trim them if vital. This promotes the formation of latest roots.

Add New Soil: Fill the bottom of the extremely-modern pot with a layer of clean potting soil. Place the plant inside the middle and cover it with soil, leaving a place of about an inch under the rim.

After transplanting, water the plant lightly to allow the soil settle and flush out air bubbles.

Care Post-Transplant: For a few days, place the plant in oblique light; do no longer fertilize proper away. After every week, bypass returned in your normal care time desk.

Tips for Success: Always use potting soil this is appropriate for the shape of plant.

To protect the roots from damage and marvel, be slight with them.

Remove any damaged or overly prolonged roots to sell healthful development.

To reduce stress in the course of the transplantation process, water the plant first.

If relocating the plant to a place with considerably converting illumination, adapt it to its new surroundings grade by grade.

Final Thoughts: Any plant proprietor want for you to transplant and repot their plant life. Your vegetation will live longer and be more colourful in case you regularly observe them and provide them the attention they need. Keep in mind that most plant life are rather hard and will benefit hundreds from a well performed transplant or repotting method, notwithstanding the truth that the approach may additionally additionally appear frightening.

four.2 Watering Techniques and Drainage

For houseplants to stay wholesome and thrive, right watering techniques and remarkable drainage are critical. An thorough summary of each features is furnished under:

Watering Techniques:

Observe Plant Needs: The amount of water that numerous plants need varies. While some flourish in barely drier situations, others name for dependably moist soil. Recognize the excellent necessities of your flora to prevent both overwatering or underwatering.

Finger Test: About an inch of earth need to be touched collectively together with your finger. Water is needed if the soil seems dry. Delay watering if the soil is still wet. This brief check aids in keeping off overwatering.

Water Thoroughly: Make positive the complete root ball is submerged in water even as you water. The root region should be nicely-saturated while you water to the factor wherein more water is draining from the bottom of the pot.

Bottom Watering: The plant will acquire moisture from the soil via the drainage holes in the pot in case you submerge it in a saucer of water. This may additionally moreover stop water from gathering on top of the soil, that may bring about root rot.

Avoid Standing Water: Never depart pots submerged in water for an extended amount of time. Root rot may additionally give up result if the roots are suffocated in this manner.

Time of Day: If in any respect viable, water vegetation inside the morning. This lowers the opportunity of fungus issues thru permitting greater moisture on leaves to dry out at a few degree inside the day.

Use Room Temperature Water: While heat water can also consist of minerals that would harm plant life, cold water shocks plant roots. Water at room temperature is proper.

Drainage:

Importance of Drainage: Water need to now not increase at the lowest of the pot due to the truth this could cause root rot and distinct fungi ailments. It guarantees that more water is taken out of the idea location.

Use Well-Draining Soil: Pick a potting aggregate that is especially formulated for the sort of plant you're planting. To increase drainage, those mixtures frequently encompass additives like perlite, vermiculite, or sand.

Select the Right Pot: Make notable the bottom of your pots has drainage holes. As a end result, extra water could in all likelihood evaporate and air can get to the roots. Consider placing a plastic nursery pot indoors decorative pots within the occasion that they do not have drainage holes.

Elevate Pots: To beautify pots a touch bit off the saucer, place them on pot feet, bricks, or stands. This stops the pot from becoming submerged in water.

Use Adequate Pot Size: Don't use pots which is probably heaps large than what the plant desires. Overwatering is much more likely while there may be too much soil for the cause that it may keep extra moisture than the plant goals.

Add Drainage Materials: Before which includes soil, lay down small stones or shards of damaged pottery at the lowest of the pot. By doing so, you offer some other layer wherein water can collect and forestall soil from blocking the drainage holes.

Monitor Drainage: In order to growth drainage after watering, you would possibly need to make modifications to the potting mix or the field itself.

Keep in mind that the specifics of watering and drainage may additionally moreover range depending on the fashion of plant and its surroundings. Assess the fitness of your plant life frequently, and make any adjustments to your watering time table. You'll advantage a deeper comprehension in their requirements with time.

four.Three Fertilizing for Healthy Growth

A vital part of sustaining healthy development in houseplants is fertilizing. It offers vegetation the vital nutrients they require to thrive, making up for any deficiencies of their increase environment. To preserve the health of your indoor flora, don't forget the subsequent complete assessment of fertilizer techniques:

Understanding Nutrient Needs: The nutrient necessities of severa vegetation vary. Nitrogen (N), phosphorus (P), and potassium (K) are the three vital macronutrients that flora require; the ones ratios are often decided on fertilizer labels. In smaller quantities, trace elements like iron, copper, and zinc, further to secondary vitamins like calcium, magnesium, and sulfur, also are critical.

Choosing the Right Fertilizer:

Fertilizers are available a whole lot of office work, collectively with liquid, granular, and sluggish-launch formulations. Pick a fertilizer based totally definitely honestly on the necessities and diploma of increase of your vegetation. Balanced fertilizers, like 10-10-10, are effective for giant preservation, at the same time as distinctiveness formulations, like excessive-phosphorus for flowering, are designed to cope with particular increase levels.

Frequency and Timing:

During their active growing seasons, frequently in spring and summer season, houseplants need fertilization. For records on application frequency, check with the label. It's important to keep away from immoderate applications of fertilizer because of the reality doing so can bring about nutrient imbalances, root burning, and slow growth.

Dilution and Application:

To avoid overfeeding when the usage of liquid fertilizers, dilute them to 1/2 of or a fourth of the prescribed power. Avoid getting liquid fertilizers at the plant's leaves by means of using them at once to the soil. Distribute granular fertilizers uniformly over the soil's ground, then quick rub down them into the pinnacle layer.

Pre-watering and Application:

It's a terrific idea to water your vegetation earlier than fertilizer is used. This reduces the possibility of unfavourable the plant's roots with targeted vitamins and aids in the fertilizer's even distribution at some level inside the soil.

Avoiding Fertilizer Buildup:

Salt buildup within the soil can prevent end end result from the buildup of wasted minerals over the years. This can also restrict the uptake of vitamins and injure plant roots. To avoid this, water the soil nicely on a ordinary foundation until the surplus water drains from the bottom of the pot.

Organic vs. Synthetic Fertilizers:

As they decompose, herbal fertilizers slowly release vitamins, ensuring a ordinary deliver over time. They additionally enhance the microbial activity and soil shape. On the alternative facet, artificial fertilizers offer authentic dietary ratios and quicker effects. You should make a desire depending for your alternatives and the desires of the plant.

Monitoring and Adjusting:

Pay attention to how fertilizing affects your flowers. You may be overfertilizing in case you see leaf burn, stunted growth, or discoloration. Growth this is slow and faded-searching leaves need to suggest nutrient shortage. You want to consequently regulate your fertilization agenda.

Winter Dormancy:

During the wintry climate, an entire lot of houseplants go through a section of restricted boom. It's terrific to reduce or quit fertilization proper now. As fast due to the fact the flora begin to make bigger all once more inside the spring, start feeding them again.

Fertilizing Different Types of Plants:

Look into the perfect requirements of your houseplants. While positive flowers, like cactus and succulents, call for sparingly implemented fertilizer, others, like tropical plants, might also moreover moreover advantage from more frequent feeding.

Keep in mind that fertilization is great one issue of plant maintenance. Your indoor plants' cutting-edge health and boom are inspired thru a variety of factors, which encompass adequate lights, everyday watering, proper drainage, and best temperatures. You may moreover additionally modify your fertilizing ordinary for the great results thru preserving a regular eye for your plants and being receptive to their goals.

Chapter 9: Maintaining Healthy Houseplants

five.1 Pruning and Trimming Tips

For houseplants to live healthy and appealing, pruning and trimming are vital techniques. These techniques entail the elimination of particular plant additives, such as leaves, stems, and branches, so that you can sell healthful improvement, enhance aesthetics, and shield towards disease. Here are wonderful commands for reducing and pruning indoor vegetation:

Tools and Materials:

To make precise cuts, use smooth, nicely-stored pruning shears or scissors.

Before and after usage, disinfect your gadget to stop the spread of infection.

Know Your Plant:

Study each plant species' precise necessities because of the truth distinct plant life require fantastic trimming strategies.

While some flora absolutely want a piece pruning, others advantage from everyday trimming to preserve their shape.

Timing:

When a plant is actively developing, commonly within the spring or early summer season, prune. When the plant is dormant, avoid intense pruning.

At any time of the one year, remove any damaged or useless leaves.

Deadheading:

To inspire the plant to attention energy on developing new blooms, often eliminate spent plants.

Remove Diseased or Damaged Parts:

To save you illnesses and pests from spreading, remove any leaves which are discolored, yellowing, or damaged.

Encourage Bushier Growth:

To sell branching and deliver the idea that the department is fuller, pinch or trim the hints of latest branches.

Shape and Size Control:

Maintain the plant's supposed period and form through pruning. To inspire a greater compact shape, get rid of immoderate or straggly boom.

When shaping, preserve in mind the plant's natural improvement sample. Some vegetation need a greater loose-shape, natural look.

Remove Suckers and Water Sprouts:

Water sprouts seem from the number one stems, whereas suckers sprout from the plant's base. To divert energy towards more healthy growth, dispose of those.

Prune for Airflow:

To enhance airflow inside the plant, thin out busy regions. This helps normal plant health and aids within the prevention of fungal infections.

Avoid Drastic Pruning:

To keep away from wonder and stress, do not reduce off more than one-1/3 of the plant's foliage without delay.

Prune Leggy Growth:

If your plant begins offevolved to sag (have prolonged, flimsy stems), reduce it again to a more potent node to sell new development.

Propagation:

Cuttings may be used to propagate a few flora. To begin new plant life, trim healthy stems and plant them in soil or water.

Prune Plants at Their Roots:

If the roots are encircling the inspiration ball, lessen them again in advance than repotting. In the present day-day region, this promotes root growth this is greater wholesome.

Observation and persistence

Keep an eye fixed on how your plant reacts to pruning. It should make the effort in advance than you examine outcomes due to the reality no longer all flowers require the same approach.

Frequent Maintenance:

Regular mild pruning frequently yields higher effects than sporadic heavy pruning. This receives rid of the requirement for intense movement.

Before pruning or trimming, hold in mind that each plant has particular dreams, for that reason it's far critical to discover about and understand the ones needs. When executed well, these strategies can sell plant increase and enhance the aesthetic enchantment of your indoors environment.

five.2 Pest and Disease Management

Managing pests and illnesses is crucial for keeping your houseplants wholesome and colourful. If those problems are not steady proper away, they might rapid amplify and injure human beings critically. Here is a thorough description of a way to manipulate sicknesses and pests on indoor flora:

Prevention:

Healthy Environment: Begin with healthy flowers and maintain a positive putting. The herbal defenses of plant life are strengthened with the resource of manner of suitable hydration, lighting fixtures, and air movement.

Introduce glowing flowers after a time of isolation to save you the spread of any infections.

To decrease the amount of regions in which pests and illnesses may likely cover, regularly easy and take away fallen plants, vain leaves, and great debris.

To stop soil-borne ailments from getting into the pots, use sterilized potting soil.

Identification:

Regular Inspection: Check your plant life frequently for signs and symptoms of illnesses or pests. Examine the plant for ordinary stains, discolouration, wavy boom, sticky residue, or physical pests.

Reference Resources To help in identifying commonplace pests and illnesses, preserve to be had plant-particular references or on-line assets.

Common Pests and Diseases:

These sap-sucking insects, alongside aspect aphids, mealybugs, and scale bugs, damage plant life and release sticky honeydew that might inspire the spread of mould.

Spider mites are tiny bugs that purpose leaves to stipple and produce skinny webbing, which discolors the leaves.

Fungus Gnats: Tiny flies that lay their eggs in wet soil and produce larvae that can damage roots.

White, powdery coating on leaves delivered on with the resource of a fungus is referred to as powdery mould.

Root rot is a fungus that develops because of immoderate watering and makes flowers wilt.

Treatment:

To prevent the unfold of pests or ailments, isolate diseased plant life from wholesome ones.

Trim impacted leaves and branches to dispose of the problem's starting place.

Natural Predators: Use predatory mites or helpful bugs like ladybugs to reduce pest numbers.

Use herbal remedies like neem oil and insecticidal cleansing cleansing cleaning soap to suffocate pests and modify their lifestyles cycles.

Chemical Treatments: Chemical insecticides have to quality be used as a very last hotel. To avoid terrible the plant or the surroundings, use them cautiously and consistent with the suggestions.

Cultural Practices:

Proper Watering: Refrain from overwatering due to the fact stagnant air can breed illness. To maintain leaves dry, water plants from the base up.

Proper air waft is crucial to stopping humidity buildup, which evokes the boom of fungi.

Controlling humidity: Some flora want better stages of humidity, whilst others do higher in drier environments. Adapt as essential.

Avoid over-fertilizing to save you lush increase from luring bugs.

Pruning and Thinning: Prune often to boom airflow and thin out dense boom.

Integrated Pest Management (IPM):

Monitor: Constantly observe the health and presence of pests on plants.

Identify: Correctly find out the form of pest or disorder.

Prevent: Put safeguards in vicinity to reduce vulnerabilities.

Control: Start with the least unstable solutions and progressively step up your manipulate strategies.

Evaluate: Consistently check the overall performance of your techniques.

Keep in thoughts that controlling pests and illnesses in houseplants requires persistence. You can preserve an energetic indoor lawn alive with the useful resource of using combining precautions, short reaction, and attentive remark. Don't be afraid to invite nearby gardening authorities or experts for help if a amazing hassle turns into overwhelming.

five.Three Troubleshooting Common Issues

Maintaining the fitness of your indoor vegetation and ensuring they thrive require you to troubleshoot common troubles. Here is an in depth guide that will help you in recognizing and solving exquisite issues:

Yellowing Leaves:

Overwatering: Too a excellent deal water can suffocate roots, inflicting leaves to become yellow. Before rewatering, let the pinnacle inch of soil dry out.

Underwatering: Insufficient water availability consequences in yellowing and drooping of leaves. When you could touch the top inch of dust, it's time to water.

Nutritional Deficiency: Yellowing leaves may be introduced on with the aid of a lack of vital nutrients, specifically nitrogen. Use a balanced fertilizer, if feasible.

Brown Tips:

Low Humidity: Brown recommendations on leaves might likely cease end result from inadequate humidity. Plant grouping, using a humidifier, or misting the foliage can all be beneficial.

Fluoride in Water: Fluoride can be poisonous to some plants. Use distilled water or wait 24 hours earlier than watering with tap water.

Drooping Leaves:

Underwatering: When there isn't enough water, the leaves slump. Make certain the plant is properly-tired and deliver it plenty of water.

Overwatering can bring about root rot, which reasons wilting. Trim the complicated roots and repot the plant in properly-draining soil.

Leggy increase

Lack of Light: Plants will gather for slight assets at the same time as there isn't sufficient slight. Consider transferring the plant to a greater slight-filled region or making an investment in extra develop lighting.

Falling Leaves:

Natural Loss of Hair: It's regular for some leaves to fall, mainly decrease leaves. However, pressure, immoderate watering, or pests may be responsible for excessive leaf drop.

Leaf drop can be brought on via pests like aphids and spider mites. Regularly check the plant, and if important, treat with insecticidal cleaning cleansing cleaning soap.

Mold or Mildew:

High Humidity: Too a whole lot moisture encourages the boom of fungi. Increase airflow, abstain from overwatering, and ensure plants are spaced nicely.

Poor drainage: Mold can extend in repute water. Repot the plant in a soil that drains well and prevent allowing extra water to accumulate in saucers.

No Fruits or Flowers:

Lack of Light: In order to bloom, many flowering flowers need enough mild. Make powerful they get the encouraged amount of light.

Lack of Pollination: In order for some flora to produce fruit, pollination must occur. To skip pollen from one blossom to each different, offer the plant a moderate shake or use a tiny brush.

Leaf Discoloration or Deformation:

Pests: Aphids, mealybugs, and scale bugs can distort and discolor leaves. Manually cast off pests or use the right insecticides.

Infections because of viruses or bacteria can deliver upward thrust to ordinary leaf patterns. Put the plant in quarantine to prevent the unfold of the sickness, and think about trimming any inflamed areas.

Growing Slowly:

Root-certain: The plant's boom may be inhibited if it has outgrown its discipline. Put the plant in a slightly huge field by using the usage of repotting.

Nutrient Deficiency: Growth that is stunted because of a lack of vitamins. Use a balanced fertilizer to feed the plant in accordance with its necessities.

Wilting Despite Moist Soil:

Root problems: Wilting can show up even in soil that is wet because of diseased or broken roots. Examine the roots for rot, and prune as important.

To effectively troubleshoot, it's far important to recognize the best goals of your houseplants because of the truth every type of plant has really considered one of a type requirements. Regular monitoring, suitable watering strategies, appropriate lights, and proactive pest control can all help prevent and remedy common issues.

Chapter 10: Indoor Plant Decor And Display

6.1 Creating Eye-Catching Arrangements

A a laugh technique to enhance the aesthetics and beauty of your residing environment is by means of creating attractive preparations for houseplants. When growing visually appealing plant shows, there are some of critical regulations and thoughts to hold in thoughts no matter your diploma of enjoy with flora or whether or now not you're simply getting began with indoor gardening.

Choose a Theme or Style: Choose a subject or fashion that enhances your indoors format earlier than you start arranging your houseplants. Having a topic in thoughts will assist you cut down your alternatives, whether or not or not you want a graceful, minimalist format with a few cautiously selected plant life or a lush, jungle-inspired affiliation with numerous sizes and textures.

Select Complementary Plants: Take under consideration the flora' boom styles, shades, textures, and sizes at the equal time as choosing them to your arrangement. Choose a choice of flora that work nicely together and provide aesthetic variation. Combining flowers which can be tall, cascading, and compact could likely bring about an attention grabbing association.

Container Selection: The final look is notably inspired via the container choice. Think of using an entire lot of planters, which incorporates wall-installed planters, setting baskets, terrariums, and pots. The bins' production and colour scheme have to supplement the motif you have were given picked.

Play with Heights and Levels: By changing the heights of your plant life, you can provide visible hobby. Plants have to be prepared with shorter ones on the the the front and better ones inside the rear or center. Utilize shelves or plant stands to function elevation.

Focus on Color Contrast: To produce startling contrasts, use an entire lot of foliage colorings. Plants with leaf styles need to be contrasted with people with robust hues. For the affiliation to stand out, use complementing colorations.

Texture and Form: Mixing vegetation with numerous leaf sorts and textures offers the association more intensity and individual. A compelling visible experience can be produced through contrasting smooth leaves with ones which may be prickly or difficult.

Consider Growth Rates: Pay attention to the chosen plants' fees of growth. One plant outgrowing the others and scary the equilibrium of the affiliation is not what you want to arise. It may be required to carry out normal upkeep and pruning to keep the plants beneath control.

Balance and Symmetry: A placing association need to strike a stability so you may be powerful. Asymmetrical designs can produce a more dynamic and natural appearance, whereas symmetrical ones sell order and are aesthetically tremendous.

Accessorize: Add ornamental components to the association, which encompass tiny stones, pebbles, or ornamental collectible collectible figurines. Make positive they do no longer overshadow the display and they combo in with the plants.

Lighting and Placement: Take into consideration the lighting within the location you have got were given picked to your affiliation. While some plant life decide upon low moderate, others do fantastic in direct, vivid light. Your association should be positioned in which the flora may additionally additionally develop and flourish.

Maintenance and Care: For your affiliation to maintain looking its exquisite, common safety is critical. It is essential to water, fertilize, and dust the leaves. In order to keep the deliberate design, make cautious to alter the affiliation due to the fact the flora growth.

Change with Seasons: The shifting seasons may be taken beneath consideration at the same time as updating your plant association.

The affiliation may additionally additionally continue to be captivating and new thru switching out exceptional flowers or which includes seasonal gildings like ornaments or plant life.

Keep in mind that designing attractive preparations for indoor flowers is a modern and experimental paintings shape. There is not a person approach that works for anyone, so do now not be afraid to test and alternate matters up based on your specific alternatives and the unique tendencies of the vegetation you've got were given.

6.2 Hanging and Wall-Mounted Plants

With their potential to offer a hint of greenery and aesthetic hobby to masses of locations, setting and wall-installed flora have become famous alternatives for both interior and out of doors dcor. These vegetation have specific blessings that permit individuals to make the most in their living area, deliver a piece little little bit of nature into town settings, or even beautify indoor air super.

Typically, hooks, macramé hangers, or exceptional resourceful placing gadgets are used to maintain putting plant life from the ceiling or increased homes. It is easy to discover selections that during shape masses of hobbies and environment due to the reality they'll be to be had in an entire lot of sizes, shapes, and species. Pothos, spider plant life, ferns, and trailing succulents like string of pearls are a few common options for striking plants.

Plants which is probably set up on walls hire vertical areas that would otherwise pass unused. These flora may be furnished in custom planters or perhaps on upcycled gadgets like vertical gardens, timber pallets, or frames. This form of set-up lets in the improvement of living artwork quantities that turn walls into colourful representations of nature.

Including placing and wall-installation flora for your design has a number of benefits:

Space Maximization: Hanging and wall-installation flora provide a way for human beings with restricted floor location to characteristic greenery to their environment with out giving up critical area.

Aesthetic Appeal: Any location blessings visually from flowers because they melt lines and offer texture. Plants which can be hung from the ceiling or installation on partitions can serve as accent quantities or art work well with unique format components in a area.

Improved Air Quality: By gathering carbon dioxide and freeing oxygen, vegetation decorate the first rate of the air internal houses. By removing contaminants, moreover they useful resource in air purification and make a contribution to a higher living environment.

Stress Reduction: According to research, being spherical flowers can lower pressure and growth emotions of health. It can assist create a extra tranquil environment to include them in it, even within the shape of putting or wall-installed flora.

Creativity and Personalization: Hanging and wall-installation flora can be arranged in some of strategies for individuality and creativity. To make a unique and custom designed show, human beings may additionally moreover experiment with one-of-a-kind plant kinds, preparations, and packing containers.

Connection to Nature: There can be restrained get right of entry to to nature in metropolitan regions. A way to connect to nature and bring a piece of the outdoor into indoors settings is through placing and wall-established plant life.

It's essential to hold in mind factors like slight availability, humidity stages, and the right requirements of each plant species at the same time as choosing flowers for placing or wall-established presentations. Additionally, it is critical to provide the plant life with the right care so they'll flourish of their multiplied places. Healthy placing and wall-installation plants require ordinary watering, appropriate fertilization, and coffee trimming, amongst distinctive maintenance practices.

A flexible and aesthetically attractive method to introduce nature into indoor and out of doors environments is through striking and wall-established plants. They offer numerous advantages, from higher air brilliant and reduced strain to place maximization. These installations may additionally emerge as adorable attention areas, changing any region right into a greener and greater colourful environment with the proper plant choice and upkeep.

6.3 Incorporating Houseplants into Interior Design

A popular and powerful fashion that offers a breath of fresh air to living areas is the incorporation of houseplants into indoors design. In addition to their aesthetic appeal, houseplants provide some of advantages that assist each the occupants and the surroundings as a whole. Here's an intensive exam of the way to efficiently embody indoor vegetation into indoors design:

Choose the Right Plants: Before selecting flowers, don't forget the humidity, lighting fixtures, and amount of preservation of your vicinity. Succulents flourish in vibrant, sunny places, however low-light sorts like snake plant life and pothos are brilliant for darkly lit interiors.

Aesthetic Complement: Living décor components which encompass houseplants can enhance a area's texture, color, and visible appeal. The use of huge, leafy plants as focal elements and the layering of smaller plants on cabinets or windowsills to characteristic more greenery are each options.

Enhance Ambiance: Plants add to the surroundings of a space with the resource of fostering serenity and a experience of connectedness to nature. It has been confirmed that having greenery round lets in human beings experience much less pressured and extra comfortable.

Natural Dividers: Tall flowers located with care can serve as herbal walls to separate regions in an open floor plan. This is mainly useful in loft-style homes or studio flats.

Vertical Gardens: To make use of wall vicinity, consider putting planters or vertical gardening. These installations produce a beautiful, livable artwork of artwork in addition to saving vicinity at the ground.

Scale and Proportion: Pick plants which can be suitable for the space. For example, large flowers, like mess around leaf figs, healthy better in exquisite residing rooms than smaller flora do in small bedrooms.

Contrast and Balance: Plants inside the domestic can evaluation with items artificial via human beings, in conjunction with furniture and electronics. The room is given a fascinating equilibrium via the evaluation of stiff lines and organic office work.

Color Harmony: Houseplants add greater colors than top notch green. Think approximately the colors of the leaves and the manner they complement or evaluation with the colors to your present color scheme.

Accessorizing Planters: Design elements are protected inside the pots themselves. The choice of planters can beautify the entire style, whether or no longer they'll be industrial metal tins, bohemian macramé hangers, or minimalist porcelain pots.

Biophilic Design: The dating amongst humans and the natural global is emphasized on this format concept. The use of houseplants promotes comfort and properly-being and is a wonderful suit with biophilic layout thoughts.

Layering and Grouping: Plants which may be each at the floor, on cabinets, or suspended from the ceiling can be organized at various heights to feature depth. Plants of various heights and shapes may be grouped collectively to create attractive groupings.

Functionality: Aloe vera and lavender are two examples of indoor flowers which have realistic uses. While lavender has a calming fragrance, aloe vera is extensively recognized for its recuperation competencies.

Seasonal Rotation: Think approximately turning plant life according with their increase and seasonal changes. This now not only continues the location looking new, however additionally makes effective the plant life get the right quantity of slight and interest.

Maintenance Considerations: Including indoor vegetation calls for self-control to their upkeep. Consider your abilities to preserve the vegetation; if you have a busy life, pick out low-maintenance ones.

Personalization: Your individual and pursuits can be pondered inside the houseplants you choose out. The flora you choose out can display statistics about you, whether or no longer or not you have got were given a penchant for robust cacti or are drawn to unusual orchids.

More than actually placing flowers in an area, interior layout consists of houseplants. It entails carefully integrating them into the cultured of the region as a whole, considering how they've an impact on the environment, and being involved for them to preserve them healthy. The surrender effect is a domestic that is warmth and restorative manner to the seamless fusion of nature and layout.

Chapter 11: Advanced Houseplant Care

7.1 Propagation Techniques

Houseplant propagation strategies entail developing new flowers from seed collected from older ones. There are numerous techniques, each of it is appropriate for specific plant sorts. Here is a thorough summary:

Seed Propagation:

Plants are raised using this approach from seeds. Due to their gradual increase, houseplants are less likely to revel in it than many outdoor vegetation, which makes feel. However, a few houseplants, at the aspect of African violets, cactus, and succulents, can be grown from seeds.

Division:

For plants that typically shape clumps or have numerous stems, use this technique. The plant is carefully taken out of the pot, and the roots are reduce into smaller quantities. Then, each phase can be potted up as a separate plant. This is a common approach for growing ferns and hostas.

Stem Cuttings:

Taking a chunk of the stem with leaves and inspiring it to root is one of the most commonplace techniques. Until roots shape, the reducing is positioned in the appropriate growth medium. For flowers like coleus, philodendrons, and pothos, this is powerful.

Leaf Cuttings:

Some plant life may be extended from a unmarried leaf. A sound leaf is taken out and set down at the developing medium. New flowers will sprout from the leaf's base. This approach can be used to propagate jade vegetation and african violets.

Root Cuttings:

This technique consists of taking a chunk of a root and stimulating it to grow into a brand new plant for flora that save energy in their roots. Plants like bamboo and snake flora are relevant for this technique.

Layering:

When layering, a flexible stem is bent to the ground, secured, after which a part of it is included with dust. When the brand new plant has superior its roots at the blanketed vicinity, it's far detached from the decide plant. Plants like spider plants can use this method.

Air Layering:

Similar to layering, however accomplished above earth. An injured stem segment is given rooting hormone treatment, wrapped in a moist medium, and protected. Within the covered location, roots shape; as speedy as robust, the modern-day-day plant is separated.

Offsets and Runners:

Some plants broaden tiny runners or offshoots that can be separated and grown as independent plants in a pot. Aloe vera offsets and spider plant runners are examples.

Bulb Division:

Amaryllis and different bulbous houseplants may be prolonged by means of decreasing bulbs into sections, every of which has a piece of the basal plate and a few scales.

Grafting:

In this cutting-edge approach, the rootstock and scion of wonderful plant life are connected on the stem. It's regularly hired to breed unusual or unusual sorts.

The accurate developing medium, timing, humidity, temperature, and the type of plant all have a characteristic in propagation success. Try out severa techniques to peer which fits your indoor flora the best.

7.2 Managing Large or Specialized Plants

Large or specialised plants want to be controlled the use of a whole strategy that considers a variety of factors, together with operational effectiveness, protection, upkeep, and organisation requirements compliance. Effective manage is critical for maximizing manufacturing and ensuring the welfare of personnel in any specialized commercial employer operation, which include production centers, electricity plants, chemical processing gadgets, and certainly one of a kind gadgets.

Planning and Organization: A entire technique inclusive of the goals, techniques, and responsibilities ought to be the first step. Establish a hierarchy of jobs and smash paintings down into digestible portions. This guarantees that everyone is privy to their obligations and makes matters run more easily.

Resource Allocation: Effectively distribute assets, consisting of labor, gadget, raw substances, and utilities. Allocating assets nicely avoids bottlenecks and decreases downtime delivered on via using shortages.

Safety: Safety want to return back first. Enforce the usage of non-public shielding device (PPE), carry out not unusual protection schooling, and put in force strict safety rules. To find out and reduce functionality risks, everyday protection audits and inspections are critical.

Maintenance: Programs for preventive and predictive safety are critical to preserve the general performance of specialised equipment and tool. Regular tests and safety help discover issues and join them in advance than they emerge as high-priced breakdowns.

Compliance and Regulations: Regulations and requirements unique to the business enterprise need to regularly be observed by means of way of specialised factories. Avoiding prison and monetary ramifications requires keeping compliance with environmental, safety, and working necessities.

Technology Integration: Include cutting-edge tools like IoT sensors, records analytics, and maintenance making plans software program. These technology can beneficial resource device optimization, downtime reduce charge, and device health monitoring.

Quality Control: Put in location a dependable excellent control machine to assure that the goods fulfill the desired necessities. Regular super inspections keep wastage and transform by using using assisting in the early detection of issues.

Supply Chain Management: Make positive that carriers and businesses are successfully coordinated if the capacity is predicated upon on a complex supply chain. Efficiency can be improved and garage fees may be decreased with without a doubt-in-time stock control.

Training and Skill Development: To help personnel beautify their abilities and live modern with market dispositions and improvements, offer ordinary training to them. Employees with higher schooling are much more likely to make a contribution to the success of the plant.

Chapter 12: Nurturing Your Green Thumb

Eight.1 Developing Observation and Care Skills

To maintain the health and vigor of your indoor inexperienced buddies, you must discover ways to look at and take care of houseplants. Even regardless of the reality that they require much less care than outdoor plant life, houseplants even though want interest, knowledge, and a pointy eye to thrive. Here is an in depth guide to help you in developing those abilties:

The Best Plants to Choose: Begin with the resource of selecting houseplants which is probably compatible together along with your diploma of dedication and the surroundings in your property. While some plant life may be extra forgiving, others need careful renovation. Think approximately such things as the quantity of moderate, the humidity, and your very own skills to maintain and water the plant.

Understand Light Requirements: The quantity of mild that diverse vegetation want varies. While some can cope with low light degrees, others thrive in direct, sturdy light. Place flora in your house taking note of the lighting fixtures patterns. Make quality they may be receiving the precise quantity of mild with the aid of the use of periodically checking in on them and adjusting their positions.

Watering Routine: Watering is one of the maximum critical additives of plant care. Establish a ordinary watering time table at the identical time as considering the character necessities of every plant. Root rot can end result from overwatering, and stress can also moreover end give up result from underwatering. Regularly check the soil's moisture content material cloth material and make any changes to your watering time table.

Learn About Humidity: Dry situations can arise indoors, particularly whilst warmers are running in some unspecified time within the future of the iciness months. There are some vegetation that require higher humidity levels, such ferns and tropical types. To preserve your flowers' humidity tiers at their quality degrees, strive misting, pebble trays, or a humidifier.

Soil Knowledge: Different styles of soil are wanted for diverse flora. Learn approximately the unique soil requirements of your indoor plants. Some growth excellent in soil that drains effortlessly, at the identical time as others do great in soil that maintains more moisture.

Pruning and Deadheading: Check your plants often for wasted blossoms and useless or yellowing leaves. To sell new increase and prevent the unfold of illnesses, eliminate these. Retrim lanky increase to promote bushier vegetation.

Fertilizing Routine: Occasionally feeding indoor vegetation will assist them get the crucial vitamins they want. Establish a fertilizer ordinary after studying approximately your plants' nutritional requirements. Avoid overfertilizing your flowers due to the fact this may damage them.

Pest and Disease Management: Watch out for any signs of pests like mealybugs, spider mites, or aphids. The key to preventing infestations is early detection. Investigate herbal or chemical remedies to remedy the ones issues without endangering your plant life.

Rotate Your Plants: To make certain that every one additives get maintain of equal publicity to mild, rotate your flowers on a ordinary basis. By doing so, uneven boom is avoided and a balanced shape is promoted.

Develop the dependancy of paying awesome hobby in your plant life. Take be privy to versions in growth, shade, and fashionable look. This allow you to in figuring out problems early and resolving them in advance than they worsen.

Study up: Each plant is special. Spend a while getting to know about the specific requirements of every of your indoor plants. You can provide the extremely good care in case you are aware about their herbal environment, boom patterns, and maintenance desires.

Keep a Care Journal: Record your plant care routine in a journal. Make a word of the dates you fertilized, at the equal time as you watered, your observations, and any changes you made. You can use this file to find out styles and manual your judgments.

Trial and Error: Learning a way to have a have a observe and deal with indoor plant life is a lifelong manner. Failures are possibilities to look at and extend your abilties; do not let them demotivate you.

Join close by gardening golf equipment or take part in online plant organizations to connect to one-of-a-kind plant fanatics. Sharing information and getting tips from seasoned plant fans can assist in fixing commonplace problems.

Houseplant care takes a capability set that consists of know-how, determination, and careful observation. You can also set up a flourishing indoor lawn that beautifies your property and adds a touch of nature by using the usage of honing those abilties.

eight.2 Experimenting with Different Plant Species

Trying out several plant species as indoor plants can be an interesting and fruitful hobby. People who want to function a touch of nature interior have a large kind of opportunities past the same old selections way to the sector of houseplants. You can also moreover upload range on your indoor region by using the use of experimenting with one in all a kind plant species and mastering approximately their outstanding textures, colorings, increase patterns, and upkeep desires.

Understanding the environmental conditions that every plant species thrives in is one of the most vital components of task experiments with numerous plant species. A plant's development and health can be considerably impacted through way of variables like air movement, temperature, humidity, and mild depth. You can studies plenty about the quality living conditions for the vegetation you are inquisitive about via investigating their native environments.

It's considerable to bear in mind that now not every plant species is suitable for indoor growing. Some might be extra hard to take care of because of sure requirements, whilst others is probably more appropriate for beginners. Consider your personal degree of gardening records and the amount of time you are inclined to decide to care while deciding on the plant life for your take a look at.

To find out the potting mixes and packing containers that produce the satisfactory boom, experimentation might also moreover entail testing out many options. While positive flowers may additionally want to do better in soil that drains efficiently, others may additionally do better in substrates that keep moisture. The growth of the plant number one and the improvement of the roots can both be stricken by the sector choice.

Additionally, watering schedules should be modified based totally on the species being grown. While some plants require intervals of time with out watering, others decide upon usually wet soil. Their fulfillment may be aided by manner of way of retaining an eye constant at the moisture degrees and getting to every plant's man or woman requirements.

Techniques for pruning and maintenance might probably range notably between species. While a few plants must advantage from routine trimming to promote bushier boom, others would probable just need a small quantity of interest. You can help maintain the plants you're experimenting with in the right shape and look by way of mastering approximately specialized pruning techniques.

In your experiments with numerous plant species, be attempting to find signs and symptoms of ailment or strain. The unfold of troubles like pest infestations or nutrient deficits can be stopped with the useful resource of early evaluation. A healthy series can be maintained via way of performing recurring inspections in your vegetation and turning into knowledgeable approximately regular troubles.

Last however now not least, recording your assessments can offer insightful information for later use. Keep song of each plant's development in a magazine, noting any adjustments to boom, flowering, or huge fitness. You can enhance your approach and benefit a better information of which plant species flourish for your indoor surroundings with the aid of manner of using retaining track of your results.

Trying out severa plant species as indoor plants is a worthwhile adventure that blends clinical curiosity and innovative experimentation. You may additionally set up a severa and flourishing indoor lawn that brings the splendor of the outdoor into your residing region with the beneficial useful resource of paying close interest to what's taking vicinity, adapting your care routines, and being eager to have a observe.

eight.Three Connecting with the Houseplant Community

For plant fanatics of all stages, getting worried with the houseplant network may be a rewarding and a laugh revel in. Since houseplants have emerge as so popular in brand new years, every online and bodily agencies have sprung up which are dedicated to these green pals. Beyond best replacing advice on how to take care of plant life, the ones companies have a wealth of advantages.

They encourage a revel in of network, provide a setting for training and private development, or perhaps present possibilities to fulfill new humans.

Using social media web websites are a number of the perfect techniques to get involved in the houseplant network. These networks are rife with profiles and companies dedicated to vegetation, in which customers can percentage their collections, observe their growth, and collaborate on issues. Interacting with posts, leaving comments, and posing queries may additionally result in useful encounters with like-minded plant fanatics. It's interesting to look the form of plant life that people very own and to examine their interactions with diverse species.

Houseplant fans often visit network plant swaps, workshops, and gardening sports, which give chances for in-man or woman connections. These gatherings are extremely good for networking similarly to education.

Due to the website visitors' shared hobby, conversations commonly generally tend to waft effortlessly, making it easy to make friends and exchange advice face-to-face. Being in near proximity to plants and one of a kind gardeners offers a bodily detail to connection this is hard to imitate on line.

For individuals who need to analyze more about their plant adventures, on-line forums and internet websites devoted to vegetation are informational gold mines. On these web sites, taking element in conversations, posing queries, and sharing evaluations can bring about deep connections with folks that percentage your pastimes.

Joining agencies and companies that concentrate on flora can offer an organized opportunity to have interaction with the community of those who keep houseplants. These companies regularly time table month-to-month meetings, plant exchanges, and educational sports. These events offer possibilities to engage with humans who've a sturdy hobby inside the worldwide of vegetation, whether they may be nearby gardening clubs or strong point succulent societies.

Building relationships within the houseplant community may possibly skip past the network or on-line environment. Connecting with like-minded those who are eager to help the environment or society may be made less tough with the aid of the usage of taking component in plant-associated charity sports, community gardening tasks, or perhaps operating together on plant-themed artwork.

In essence, putting in place relationships with people of the houseplant community is set more than definitely getting flora; it is approximately finding others who've pursuits in the identical belongings you do. These interactions can bring about lifelong friendships, individual development, and a extra love of nature. Consider accomplishing out and being absolutely immersed in the wealthy tapestry of the houseplant community whether or not or now not you're an skilled plant decide or are clearly beginning your exploration of the world of indoor flora. The encounters and bonds you shape alongside the road will in fact enhance your enjoy with plants.

Chapter 13: Even Rescue Your Houseplants

In this bankruptcy, we embark on a treasure hunt in your leafy companions, masking a spectrum of options from large retail giants to shut by way of hidden gems. Our project is plain: to manual you inside the route of assets in which you can't only find out and purchase thriving flora but moreover rescue those in want of a bit TLC.

Big Box Stores:

Big area stores, which incorporate household names like Home Depot, Lowes, Wal-Mart, Target, or even your nearby grocery stores, are incredible for each seasoned gardeners and budding plant fans. These retail giants offer a massive choice of houseplants, beginning from strong succulents to swish ferns. What makes these stores particularly appealing is their accessibility and affordability. They cater to beginners, making sure a numerous choice of novice-high-quality vegetation ranging to greater renowned plant life that you will be able to discover in case you're fortunate.

Most large area stores do not concentrate on flora by myself, and do no longer constantly provide flowers the perfect interest they need. Due to the occasional lack of accurate care or perhaps distress brought on for the duration of transportation, stores will frequently have a reduced segment for plant life in want of a chunk extra care. This offers you a super possibility to keep a few cash at the identical time as nevertheless bringing domestic a plant that has ability to grow proper right into a lovely specimen with a hint extra patience and care. Keep an eye fixed constant out for ordinary shipments, as those supply easy opportunities to find out precise and flourishing greenery for your collection.

While I in my opinion want to aid my close by, family owned plant stores, which we are able to get into in the subsequent phase, there's no denying the opportunities to buy and rescue vegetation out of your neighborhood huge box keep. So, whether or now not or now not you're at the hunt for a strong snake plant or a completely particular alocasia, the ones big container stores have some thing for everybody, making them high places on your plant-looking journey.

Chapter 14: Basic Care For Any Houseplant

Now that you've warmly welcomed those new leafy companions into your location, their properly-being will become your pinnacle priority. This economic disaster serves as your entire guide to making sure their flourishing growth of their new surroundings. We'll dive deep into the critical factors of houseplant care, leaving no leaf unturned. From facts their unique lighting needs to learning the art work of watering, we'll cowl each aspect. You'll discover about the severa style of substrates and pots to be had, empowering you to make the exceptional options for every member of your green own family. Discover a way to create and maintain most appealing humidity tiers, supplying a comfortable surroundings to your vegetation to thrive. We'll demystify the arena of fertilizers, guiding you on at the same time as and a way to feed your plant life for sturdy and colourful increase. By the surrender of this financial disaster, you'll be armed with a wealth of knowledge and sensible strategies, making sure you're nicely-organized to nurture your inexperienced circle of relatives right into a lush and thriving indoor oasis. Remember, each plant is a dwelling entity with its very personal particular wishes. There are masses of species of plant life and hundreds of facts on each one in every of them to be had. While we will cowl the most number one houseplant care in this ebook, I always endorse doing extra and particular studies to your specific houseplants needs. Just like each fingerprint is precise to a person, every houseplant has wishes just as one-of-a-type. As you delve into this financial disaster, you'll benefit the perception and confidence to understand the fundamentals of being worried for houseplants and a manner to commonly tend to them with care.

Quarantine New Plants - Ensuring a Healthy Start:

Before integrating new vegetation into your installed indoor garden, it's crucial to place into effect a short quarantine period. This precautionary degree serves as a shield, protecting your gift green own family from potential pests or ailments that can accompany the newbies.

During this preliminary duration of isolation, you'll closely show the new flowers for any symptoms and symptoms of distress or infestation. This exercising is particularly essential due to the reality vegetation, like each dwelling organisms, can occasionally convey hidden troubles, notwithstanding the fact that they appear wholesome at the surface. Pests like mites, aphids, or scale bugs, similarly to fungal infections or sicknesses, won't be immediately obtrusive upon inspection.

By quarantining new flora, you create a controlled environment that permits you to carefully take a look at their behavior and famous fitness. This length additionally gives an opportunity for the plant to acclimate to its new environment with out the delivered strain of capability infestations.

Additionally, need to you find out any problems in some unspecified time in the future of the 2-four week quarantine duration, you may take proactive steps to cope with them before introducing the modern plant for your current-day collection. This prevents the unfold of pests or sicknesses, which, if left unattended, can unexpectedly have an effect on specific flowers.

Depending for your space, this will imply setting the plant in a room some distance from distinct flora or truely putting the plant in a phase of your location, some distance from the others. If you do no longer have any greater region to quarantine your new plant, it's miles despite the fact that very essential to preserve a close to eye on them and your present day plants to make sure the whole lot is looking healthful.

Remember, a vigilant method to plant quarantine is an crucial factor of accountable plant care. It now not simplest protects your funding for your developing series but moreover contributes to the general health and nicely-being of your inexperienced own family. Taking the time to establish this exercise demonstrates your determination to fostering a thriving, pest-unfastened indoor lawn.

Lighting:

Proper lights is the cornerstone of a fulfillment houseplant care. Different plant life have diverse necessities almost about mild, and records the ones wishes is important for his or her ordinary fitness and increase. Plants have various moderate necessities due to the reality they have got superior to thrive in extraordinary ecological niches with specific slight situations. This model is cautiously tied to their herbal habitats and the way they've advanced to capture and employ mild strength for photosynthesis, that's the method with the resource of manner of which plant life convert moderate, water, and carbon dioxide into energy-rich sugars. Here, we'll discover the exceptional sorts of lighting fixtures conditions that your flora can also moreover furthermore thrive in. Please keep in thoughts which you need to constantly do your very personal studies on which type of mild is high-quality to your unique plant species to thrive in.

Direct Light: Plants that thrive in direct light require exposure to sunlight for a extensive part of the day. This technique they need to be positioned near a south or west going through window wherein they're able to get hold of the entire intensity of sunlight. Examples of flora that typically thrive in direct moderate embody Cacti and Succulents.

Indirect Light: Plants that decide upon oblique light thrive in regions with filtered or diffused sunlight hours. This is probably an area shielded thru way of curtains, or a few toes far from a window in which the sunlight hours is not as intense. Many common houseplants, which embody Spider vegetation and Pothos, fall into this class.

Bright Indirect Light: This beauty falls amongst direct and oblique mild. Plants that thrive in vibrant indirect mild want to be near a window however ought to be protected against the merciless midday sun. They advantage from dappled or filtered daylight hours, which gives the right stability of depth. Examples embody Calathea and a few species of Begonias.

Medium Indirect Light: This class is just like extremely good indirect mild but with barely a good buy much less depth. Plants that fall into this beauty can tolerate a chunk greater color and might thrive in regions that get maintain of indirect slight for max of the day. Philodendrons, and Fiddle Leaf Figs are notable vegetation to have in medium oblique mild.

Low-Light: Plants in this class are especially adaptable and may thrive in regions with minimum herbal mild. They may be placed further from home windows or in spots with indirect mild. Some famous low-mild plant life encompass Syngoniums and Peace Lilies

If you live someplace wherein natural moderate is constrained, or no longer as constant as favored, consisting of a town like Seattle, WA, expand lighting can be a beneficial alternative. These specialised artificial lights mimic the natural spectrum of daytime, providing the crucial wavelengths for photosynthesis. They are to be had in various sorts, along side fluorescent, LED, and excessive-depth discharge (HID) lighting fixtures. This permits you to create a managed environment in which flora can thrive, even in spaces with constrained get right of access to to natural daylight hours. This has demonstrated to help my very personal series of all considered considered one of a type types of houseplants thrive in a room that does not acquire any direct sunlight hours.

Understanding the lighting fixtures desires of your plant life and the way to offer it, whether or not or now not through natural moderate or grow lighting fixtures, is a key issue of ensuring their nicely-being. Tailoring the slight situations to the proper necessities of your plant collection will not exceptional help to make sure your vegetation survival, however result in healthful, colourful, and flourishing green partners.

Watering:

Providing the right amount of water is important for your vegetation' fitness. Different plants have exceptional watering desires, it is crucial to do your research and discover the first-class manner to water your plant life to make certain they thrive. Here's the manner to navigate watering on your indoor lawn.

Understanding Plant-Specific Watering Needs: Different vegetation have severa water requirements primarily based mostly on their herbal habitat and tendencies. For instance, Succulents and Cacti are tailored to arid environments and require infrequent watering, on the identical time as Ferns and tropical plants thrive in extra constantly moist conditions. Researching the precise watering desires of your flowers will help you offer them with the right amount of moisture.

Testing Soil Moisture: Checking the moisture level of the soil is a important step in determining at the same time as to water your flowers. You can do that the usage of fundamental strategies:

Moisture Meter: This handy tool lets in you to correctly measure the moisture content material of the soil. Simply insert the probe into the soil at top notch depths and examine the studying. It provides a particular indication of whether or not or now not your plant dreams watering or now not.

Finger Method: A traditional and reliable approach that includes sticking your finger about an inch or into the soil. If it feels dry at that intensity, it can be time to water. If it although feels slightly damp, keep off on watering for a chunk longer.

Methods of Watering: Different flowers advantage from one-of-a-type watering techniques. Here are a few key strategies:

Top Watering: This is the maximum not unusual approach, in which you gently pour water over the soil till it begins to empty out of the lowest of the pot. It is essential to make sure the water reaches the root area with out growing waterlogged situations.

Bottom Watering: This technique consists of setting the plant's pot in a shallow field of water and allowing it to absorb moisture from the lowest up. It's especially useful for vegetation with touchy leaves or the ones at risk of soil compaction. This is my private desired with reference to watering my plant life. It ensures that the plant most effective receives what it needs.

*Extra Tip - Using a easy bowl or box permits you to look how a bargain water the plant has soaked up and while it is ready to be taken out. You can also use a dry erase marker to mark the water diploma at the sphere whilst you first placed the plant in so you can see simply how plenty water the plant has honestly soaked up.

Sub-irrigation (Self-Watering Systems): These systems use a reservoir of water related to the plant's soil via a wick or capillary motion. This allows the plant to draw up water as desired, decreasing the risk of over-watering.

By tailoring your watering habitual to the correct goals of your flowers and the usage of those techniques, you'll create an environment in which they're capable of thrive and flourish. Remember, consistency and remark are key—monitoring your vegetation often will help you refine your watering time table through the years.

Substrate:

Substrate refers back to the cloth or medium wherein flowers are grown. It offers useful resource for the roots, holds moisture, and substances vitamins. Choosing the proper substrate is vital for the fitness and nicely-being of your plants. Here are a few not unusual forms of substrate and what they provide on your flora.

Standard Potting Soil: This is a flexible all-cause combo appropriate for a sizeable variety of houseplants. It generally consists of a balanced mixture of organic count number, like Peat Moss or compost, and mineral components for aeration and drainage, you may commonly find a big potting mixture at your nearby lawn/plant hold.

Cactus and Succulent Soil: Designed for plant life that thrive in arid situations, this mixture has a better percentage of coarse substances like sand, Perlite, or Pumice to make certain extremely good drainage. It's specially tailor-made to save you over-watering, which can be terrible to Succulents and Cacti.

There also are masses of substrate materials that you could add into your potting soil to offer your flora more blessings consisting of higher drainage, aeration, more vitamins, and water-retention. Some top notch upload-ins to your plant life substrate have to encompass:

Perlite: This slight-weight, porous cloth is derived from volcanic rock. It promotes aeration and drainage in potting mixes. Perlite prevents soil compaction and lets in roots to get proper of access to oxygen extra with out problems. This makes it an wonderful addition for vegetation that require nicely-draining soil.

Peat Moss: Sphagnum Peat Moss is a herbal, natural cloth that maintains moisture properly on the same time as however considering exact aeration. It's normally used to improve moisture retention in potting mixes. However, it's vital to apprehend of sustainable sourcing practices, as peat moss harvesting will have environmental influences

Coco Coir/Coco Husk: This is a herbal fiber extracted from coconut husks. It's an inexperienced possibility to peat moss. Coco coir and Coco Husk retains moisture efficiently and gives specific aeration. It's additionally a renewable aid, making it a sustainable preference for environmentally-conscious gardeners.

Orchid Bark: Orchid bark is a hard, nicely-draining medium made from the bark of diverse tree species. It's typically used for epiphytic orchids and different vegetation that require awesome aeration spherical their roots. Orchid bark prevents waterlogged conditions and mimics the herbal environment of those flora.

Charcoal: Horticultural charcoal is used to enhance soil aeration and absorb impurities. It's mainly useful for terrariums and closed-box gardens, in which it lets in hold a healthy root surroundings by using stopping mildew and micro organism boom.

Vermiculite: Vermiculite is a mineral that expands even as heated, developing a moderate-weight, moisture-maintaining cloth. It's typically introduced to potting mixes to improve water retention. Vermiculite moreover offers aeration, making it a treasured component for flora that pick continually moist situations.

Pumice: Pumice is a volcanic rock that's been processed to remove more moisture. It's light-weight and porous, supplying high-quality aeration and drainage. Pumice is often applied in Succulent and Cacti mixes, in addition to for flowers that require well-draining soil.

Some plant life were located to thrive in opportunity substrates together with LECA (Lightweight Expanded Clay Aggregate) or Pon.

LECA (Lightweight Expanded Clay Aggregate): LECA is made through the usage of heating clay pellets, causing them to increase. You will frequently hear people inside the plant community relate them to "coco puffs" due to their brown "puffed" appearance. It's a flexible substrate that gives each aeration and moisture retention. LECA is frequently utilized in hydroponic and semi-hydroponic systems, in addition to for orchids and one of a kind epiphytic flowers. While some humans like to comprise LECA into their soil/substrate, many plant life will thrive in LECA on my own.

Pon: Pon is a synthetic substrate that mimics herbal materials like tree fern fiber. It gives splendid moisture retention and aeration, making it perfect for flowers that require steady humidity ranges, collectively with tropical ferns and mosses. Similarly to LECA, many plant proprietors have determined that their flora or perhaps cuttings thrive and root incredible in Pon by myself.

Choosing the right substrate relies upon on the ideal wishes of your vegetation and the environment they're developing in. By understanding the houses of diverse substrates, you may create a conducive environment that permits healthy root growth and traditional plant well-being.

Plant Pots:

Choosing the proper pot is as critical as deciding on the proper soil to your plant life. Different pots provide numerous benefits based totally on your plant's desires and your watering behavior. Here are the precise types of pots and their blessings.

Pots with Drainage Holes: These are the most not unusual shape of pots and are alternatively encouraged for optimum plant life. They allow excess water to break out from the bottom, stopping the soil from turning into waterlogged. This lets in to keep away from root rot and particular moisture-related problems. Pots with drainage holes additionally offer higher aeration for the roots

Pots with out Drainage Holes: These pots are usually used as ornamental outer packing containers (cache pots) for flora in plastic or nursery pots. While they'll be visually attractive, if you do no longer use them as a cache pot, they require greater care to avoid over-watering. It's critical to be aware about watering and ensure that excess water does not accumulate at the lowest with nowhere to transport. If you are absolutely set on a pot and no longer the use of a drainage holes, I should recommend the use of it as a cache pot OR I even have moreover determined collectively with rocks to the lowest of the pot offers the water someplace to take a seat down apart from growing a pool of dust at the lowest of the pot. This isn't a foolproof method, but is a nice precaution if you have no unique alternatives.

Nursery Pots: These are famous plastic pots which can be to be had numerous sizes. They typically have drainage holes and are slight-weight, making them smooth to transport and re-pot. It additionally makes backside watering, as we said above lots less tough. Nursery pots are wonderful for initial planting and for vegetation which can want to be transplanted as they enlarge.

Pots with Built-in Drainage Tray: These pots have an linked tray or saucer at the bottom to entice more water that drains out. While the ones pots provide a elegant answer for people who need their plant life to have an appealing however realistic pot, they despite the fact that require a bit little little bit of caution almost approximately watering. Generally, built in saucers aren't very massive and might with out troubles spill over if over-watered, which could motive a messy puddle to easy up. Pots with built-in trays are top notch for plant life that choose to be stored constantly wet.

Chapter 15: The Wonderful World Of Propagation

In this chapter, we'll discover the charming paintings of propagation, a expertise that lets in you to multiply the one that you love plant life and amplify your green oasis. You'll have a look at the ins and outs of what propagating involves and discover a number of the only strategies to propagate your plant life. From water propagation to using a prop field, we'll cover it all, together with treasured pointers to make certain a hit propagation ventures.

What is Propagating?

Before we dive into the techniques, it's vital to understand the concept of propagation. Simply put, propagation is the approach of creating new flowers from contemporary-day ones. This can be completed with the aid of way of taking cuttings, dividing the plant, or encouraging it to supply seeds. It's a worthwhile business enterprise that now not high-quality multiplies your plant series but moreover allows you to percent the splendor of nature with pals and fellow plant fanatics.

Most Common Ways to Propagate:

Water Propagation: This method consists of setting plant cuttings in water until they broaden roots. It's a well-known and visually attractive way to have a look at the inspiration boom method. Ideal for vegetation like Pothos, Spider flora, and Philodendrons. I clearly have placed that the majority of my plant life do super propagating in water, as long as they've got a node.

Moss Propagation: Moss propagation uses Sphagnum Moss as a growing medium for cuttings. This approach permits preserve moisture ranges and offers a supportive environment for root development. I definitely have positioned personal fulfillment using a aggregate of Sphagnum Moss and Perlite in a propagation field to root cuttings.

Perlite Propagation: Perlite, a mild-weight, porous medium, is used to root cuttings. Its extraordinary aeration houses sell wholesome root increase. Perlite propagation is particularly beneficial for vegetation that require nicely-draining situations.

Division Propagation: Division propagation is a method of asexual plant propagation that involves keeping aside a mature plant into or more sections, each of that could make bigger independently into a modern plant. This technique is usually used for plant life that glaringly expand in clumps or have more than one stems emerging from a applicable element. By dividing the plant, you create smaller, self-retaining sections, each with its very very very own root gadget.

www.ingramcontent.com/pod-product-compliance
Lightning Source LLC
Chambersburg PA
CBHW070555010526
44118CB00012B/1327